BAD CALL

BAD CALL

A Summer Job on a
New York Ambulance

MIKE SCARDINO

Little, Brown and Company

New York Boston London

Little, Brown and Company
Hachette Book Group
1290 Avenue of the Americas, New York, NY 10104
littlebrown.com

First Edition: July 2018

Little, Brown and Company is a division of Hachette Book Group, Inc. The Little, Brown name and logo are trademarks of Hachette Book Group, Inc.

The publisher is not responsible for websites (or their content) that are not owned by the publisher.

The Hachette Speakers Bureau provides a wide range of authors for speaking events. To find out more, go to hachettespeakersbureau.com or call (866) 376-6591.

ISBN 978-0-316-46961-6
LCCN 2018939632

10 9 8 7 6 5 4 3 2 1

LSC-C

Printed in the United States of America

*To Barbara, who has shown me all the best
things life has to give, every day of my life.*

*To all of you I wanted to save but couldn't.
Believe me, I tried.*

CONTENTS

CONTENTS

CONTENTS

BAD CALL

HOW BAD COULD IT BE

May 1967

NEXT WEEK I start my summer job working on St. John's Queens Hospital ambulance. I have to do this to pay for Vanderbilt.

All Mom and Dad have done since I started school last fall is complain about how expensive it is. I told them I would go to Queens College. I told them Vanderbilt was too expensive for us. I told them I didn't want to pay to join a fraternity, either, but every time I tell them I'll quit, Mom says, *Oh no, no, you need to be in a fraternity.* This is the most bizarre good-cop, bad-cop game I've ever heard of. The good cop and the bad cop are the same cop.

She's the one who wanted to go to Vanderbilt. She's the one with the friends and family in Nashville. She could have gone to Vanderbilt herself. But she lived within walking distance and wanted to be a resident student instead of a townie. So rather than commute, she refused to go at all. For years she told the story another way, that her father

3

wouldn't let her go to college, period. So much for that. I hate to think that she wants me to go there so she can have bragging rights with her old pals in Nashville. Pride does have its price. And it looks like I'm the one who'll be picking up the tab.

Everybody expects me to become a doctor. They think I'll just go to Vanderbilt and move right on into its medical school, and that will be that. They have no idea that I'm already doing so poorly at school that any med school at all is a very dim prospect, much less Vanderbilt's—which takes a minuscule percentage of its own undergraduates. I can understand that. It's a good policy. I just didn't know about it before I enrolled. I didn't know about *anything* before I enrolled. Nobody on either side of the family ever went to college.

Dad has had the St. John's ambulance account for gas and repairs for a few years. I already know most of the guys who work there pretty well. Pete, the boss, lives not far from us in Bayside. Dad talked to him, and I'm in. Just like that. No one ever actually asked me, of course. It was a done deal by the time I heard about it.

At eighteen, I'm not old enough to legally have the job. You have to be twenty-one to get a New York State chauffeur's license—which you need to drive an ambulance or a cab or a light commercial truck. So I probably won't be driving. Much. But no one seems concerned about me working as an attendant. I guess if you can enlist in the army at seventeen and see your friends get wasted in Vietnam, eighteen isn't too young to deal with total strangers getting wasted in the borough of Queens.

I'll be working fifty-six hours a week: forty straight time and sixteen at time and a half. Nights and days, whenever they need me. That's good money, and it's supposedly a plum job, by New York ambulance standards. It will pay for my tuition *and* Mom's pride in full, every summer—as long as I have to do it, which may be a long time. Unless my academic performance continues the way it's been going, in which case there'll be no more college to pay for.

Do you want to know what I think. I'll tell you anyway. I think I'd rather be a Queens College student and have no financial Sword of Damocles hanging over me and be able to relax and enjoy myself during the summers. I haven't had a real summer vacation since I was thirteen, when Dad first put me to work in the gas station.

I feel like I'm going to end up with my salad days wilting before my eyes.

I'd leave Vanderbilt and enroll in Queens College in a minute if it weren't for the fact that I met Barbara the third day at school, and we intend to marry when this—whatever *this* is—is all over. I know I said pride has its price.

I suspect love is at least as costly. Or even more.

So here I am. I can't quit premed because Dad believes college is a trade school, and I might as well not go at all if it's not to learn a trade.

5

I can't leave Vanderbilt because I'm in love.

I can't quit college at all, because I'll almost certainly end up in Vietnam.

So I'm going to work on a New York City ambulance. Wonderful. I've heard a lot of the guys' stories already. If you want to know the truth, I'm afraid. I admit it. I'm afraid, and I feel trapped, and I feel angry.

I feel like I have a fucking gun to my head, a fucking knife at my throat, and fucking shackles on my legs. Well, so much for all that. I have to do it.

How bad could it be.

FIRST DAY ON THE JOB

FIRST DAY ON the job and so far, so good. I've been on another couple of calls before—ride-alongs with Pete, the boss, and Jim, one of the drivers. A man with D.T.'s and an elderly woman who died in her sleep, in that order. But today, it's a full twelve-hour shift, and I'm on for real. I've been on since 5:30 a.m., and we haven't had a single call.

Maybe this won't be as bad as I thought.

It's lunchtime now, and we're dining in the ambulance and we get a radio call in Sunnyside. It's a *possible* DOA. I'm told DOAs always come through like that—as *possible*. Even when we go there and see the corpse for ourselves, we can only write down *Apparent DOA* on the pink sheets we use to document calls. Only a licensed MD can officially pronounce someone dead.

I'm told they once got a possible DOA that was a skeleton in a closet in a building being razed on Welfare Island.

I am partnered up with Big Al. I've actually known him for a couple of years already, as a customer at Dad's gas station. He and I are double-parked in the running ambulance near Roosevelt Avenue behind a public school, right up against a Sabrett's hot-dog cart. Al is running a weenie tab. The hot-dog man is handing them through the open window to Al as fast as he can snuggle them into their warm buns. No sauerkraut, no mustard, nothing that could slow the flow. As far as Big Al is concerned, these dogs are so good they don't need any enhancements. I agree.

Al is passing me one Sabrett's for every three he eats, usually in two bites. Al is enormous. Easily over three hundred. I don't have the nerve to ask him his weight outright. His entire football-shaped torso is hard as a rock, but not in a good way. I often think he wears some sort of support garment, like a corset, that firms him up like that.

Al likes to intimate that he's *connected* at a low level—the kind of *un*made man that sells watches out of car trunks and other stuff that *falls off the trucks*. The final link in the wise-guy marketing chain: direct to consumer. Sometimes I wonder if his underlayment might be a bulletproof vest.

The lenses in his specs are as thick as the proverbial Coke-bottle bottoms, and there is almost always the stub of a Palumbo or Di Napoli cigar, made from grade C or D tobacco, sticking out of the corner of his mouth. The kind Clint Eastwood smokes in the spaghetti westerns. They stink like hell when they're lit—hence the nickname

Guinea Stinkers. I smoke a lot—at least two packs a day—but I'm not eager to try one of those, just yet.

Anyway, Big Al's girth and the glasses and the cigar, not to mention the fact that he can be as funny as anybody I've ever met, combine to give him a sort of zany Merry Mafioso persona.

On a more sobering note, he did tell me once that if I ever wanted anyone *taken care of* to just let him know. Sure will, Al.

By the time we saddle up and hit the lights, he has inhaled twelve Sabrett's hot dogs. I have no doubt he could eat twelve more and perhaps twelve more after that. But we have to get going.

We stop near some train tracks. There's a Long Island Railroad work crew and several patrol cars and some cops and a couple of plainclothes. It's hot and I'm starting to regret the four hot dogs I've eaten. I'm sweating profusely.

We make our way to a clump of police standing over the *possible* decedent. I squeeze through to take a look. It's a young black male, semi-recumbent, head cocked back over a small canvas bag, mouth and eyes wide open, the latter pointed right at the sun. He and his clothes are drenched in perspiration. He's *apparently* dead. I enter that information on my pink sheet.

What happened is a mystery. His lunch is beside him: a substantial meatball hero and a large bottle of Coca-Cola. He had only eaten a few bites of the hero and barely touched the Coke. Did he choke. Have a heart attack. Whatever it was, it was *something*. Pretty sure he wasn't done in. Even more sure we'll never know what it was.

A couple of the LIRR guys come by and say this was the guy's first (*and last,* one volunteers with a snicker) day on the job, and he seemed like an okay guy and everyone just thought he was taking a brief lunchtime lie-down until he didn't get up. Well. First day on the job for both of us.

I hope I have better luck than he's had.

Idle chitchat ensues, cop and ambulance shoptalk: *What's your favorite precinct; Jeez, it's hot; Nice shoes. Nice shoes* goes like this: *Nice shoes. Where'd you get 'em.* To which the answer is inevitably, *DOA.*

Big Al volunteers that if we want shoes, he can get us anything we want.

Al tells me we're waiting for the crime-scene guys and the ME's—medical examiner's—truck. But it turns out we don't really have to wait. We're clear to go. Ambulances are for the living. Besides which, with a suspicious death in a public place, they almost never take away a body—that's for the ME guys.

But we don't have a call on deck, and the inertia of a really hot day plus a Sabrett's overload is upon us, so we just kind of hang around. I'm staring blankly at the body when I notice something. One by one, the fattest, brightest bluebottle flies I've ever seen are landing on the dead guy's face and then hopping into his mouth and disappearing down his throat.

This is startling and fascinating—and I guess it more or less proves he didn't choke. Where are these flies headed. I had expected this, seeing flies (and their wriggly babies) on the dead, but I'm looking at this scene and I'm surprised by the bluebottle flies. I've been told that most of the flies one sees on bodies are houseflies, and they like to congregate around the eyes or open wounds to lay their eggs and maybe have a bite or poop and then take off.

I'm standing here, and I find myself counting the blue-green beauties going into the man's mouth. Not one is coming out. I am up to thirty, and there are still more taking the plunge. I have no idea how many went down before I got here or started counting. There may well be more than fifty flies in his stomach and esophagus. Maybe even more than that. A hundred. Who knows.

As I stand here in the sun, my mind is beginning to wander. I'm trying to picture what the flashy, chubby flies are up to in there. Are they all the way into his stomach. How can they all fit. Each one is nearly the size of a peanut. What's the volume of fifty flies compared with four Sabrett's. How can they breathe in there. Are they past the stomach. Why aren't any coming out. Are they going to keep going until they come out his rear end. *Yuck.*

I've stopped counting to make room to think about the flies' itinerary. Now I'm getting a notion that maybe I should get out of the sun, because I've got this deranged urge to poke this young man's stomach to see if flies come buzzing out—like poking a hornet's nest with a stick. Like some kind of real-life Looney Tunes scenario.

What would it sound like, I wonder, if I rhythmically pressed on his abdomen. Could I make some sort of buzzing fly music. Would it be like CPR, except that he would exhale flies instead of carbon dioxide.

I've begun to think I am hallucinating until I am startled out of my lunatic fantasies by a firm poke in the back. Big Al says, *Let's go*.

He's ready for his afternoon feeding.

THE RULE OF NINES

I'VE BEEN AT St. John's several weeks now and have spent some of that time working with Jim, one of the nicest people you'd ever want to meet. When I haven't been working with Jim, I've been working with Pete, the boss. If this job were a salad, Jim would be the extra-virgin olive oil, and Pete would be the bargain-priced, horribly astringent red-wine vinegar.

I went on my second call with Jim—an unpaid ride-along before I started full-time. My call with Jim was a DOA. It was an extremely old woman who had died overnight, in her own bed, in a house she shared with her grown son and his wife.

Until then, I had only seen two dead people. That was on Thirty-Ninth Avenue, in Bayside, on my way to the deli for my mother. I was seven. It was a very bad accident, very bloody. Two old people had hit a tree. The driver, a man, had been decapitated. A woman was dead beside him. What

I remember most is there were no other people around—it was very quiet—and I had no emotional reaction.

That first call with Jim was a little bit like that. It was very quiet and I had no reaction. The dead woman had that grotesque dead-person look on her face: mouth wide open, head back, eyes slightly open. Her dentures were in a glass by the bed. Their absence turned her gape into a macabre abyss.

I was just there to look and learn. Jim really had it down, what to say and do. He was asking her family questions.

How old was she. She was ninety-eight.

Bless her heart, said Jim. *God bless her.*

He was smiling and moving his head slowly from side to side as if to underline his blessing with Don't we all wish we could go like her, at ninety-eight, in our sleep. I watched the family. They smiled, too. It was all very calming. I know it made them feel good. It made me feel good, too, and I wasn't even part of the family.

I learned a lot about patter from Jim. I feel almost certain he must have kissed the Blarney Stone at some point in his life. He is very Irish, in the very best sense. There's a lilt to his voice when he speaks. He's what the Irish call *a darlin' man.* Genuinely friendly and totally imperturbable.

Jim is actually working two jobs. The ambulance is one, and in his *spare* time, he's an electrician. He must be making a small fortune.

I would like to work only with Jim, but he can't always work. He has a bad back problem, which hits him without warning. Sometimes when he bends over, his back locks, leaving him in excruciating pain and unable to straighten out. If this happens on the job, St. John's sends out the other ambulance to pick him up.

Why they keep him on or why he wants to stay at St. John's is a mystery to me. Having a bad back on this job is like being a blind umpire. You really should consider doing something else.

Anyway, I'd like to work with Jim most of the time, but he just isn't around enough. Besides, he always works week-days, and I have to work nights and weekends or anytime they need me, which looks like it's going to be just about all the time.

It's a nice day today, not too hot. Summer's just getting into full swing. Still not the Fourth of July, but it's coming up in a couple of weeks. Jim and I get a call. It's a cop down. This could mean anything from a gunshot to getting hit in traffic, Jim says.

No matter what, *officer down* calls are always a rush. Last week, we were all outside the emergency room smoking and joking when the heavy double doors literally exploded outward, missing me by inches. Two cops burst through, on their way to an *officer down, all units respond* call.

I guess if you want to see the doughnuts fly, that's the call that will do it.

This call is behind a private house in Maspeth, right up Fifty-Seventh Avenue, not even as far as the gas tanks. It will only take us a couple of minutes to get there. And here we are. And so are the cops. Three cars.

Come around back, beckons one of the policemen. I'm expecting to see a man down, blood spurting from a gunshot wound. It's never what you think you're going to see.

Instead, a very calm man in shorts and a T-shirt is sitting on the grass with his legs splayed apart in an odd way. He's sitting in front of a charcoal grill. The coals are lit. He's obviously in distress, but he's in control. He's okay enough to tell us what happened. It's pretty simple if a bit unbelievable.

He was squirting charcoal lighter on the coals, and the can blew up, dousing his legs in burning fluid. That's it. So this can actually happen. They tell you not to do this on the can. I've done it many times.

Not no more.

He really doesn't look that bad. His legs aren't even red. But they don't look right. They look very white, almost like they're made of alabaster or something. I know what it is. They look like the fat you see on uncooked steak. Thick, opaque white fat. On the side of each leg there's a thin red line of blood, marking where the epidermis was burned back.

Jim sees me looking and takes me aside so the patient won't hear. *Those are third-degree burns.* I am surprised. Not at all what I expected, not having seen third-degree burns yet. What did I expect. Yes, blackened charred flesh. Jim contin-

16

ues, *The tissue is dead, there's no blood. The burns are deep. These are serious burns,* he goes on. *It's about the rule of nines.* I know about this but haven't memorized it. Jim gives me the Cliff's Notes.

When they give a burn victim's condition as having a certain percentage of burns over his body, it's totaled up by units of 9 percent. For example, each whole leg is 18 percent. The front of each leg would be 9 percent. Our patient has the front of both legs burned, so he has third-degree burns on 18 percent of his body.

That doesn't sound like much to me, but Jim is concerned. He gets very quiet when he's concerned, and the blarney stops cold. Apparently this percentage is very serious when the burns are third degree. Nothing to do but get this poor guy back to St. John's. Straight shot down Fifty-Seventh and right on Queens Boulevard, and we're there.

We don't usually expect any closure on calls. We get so many, there's no way to keep track. Plus we don't really want to know most of the time. And, of course, patient information is supposed to be confidential, unless you're a member of the family. But sometimes we find out anyway.

Word comes down the next day that our policeman patient has died. With third-degree burns that didn't look like anything, over just 18 percent of his body. It's so hard to believe. Maybe he died from a heart attack or some other complication. It doesn't make sense—18 percent is just a number. It just doesn't seem like that much.

But I guess it was enough.

THE NAPOLEON

I CAN'T SAY for sure exactly where we are, except that we're way up in Astoria. We got this call: woman down. What does that mean. *Down.* Could mean anything, really.

What is this place. Looks like an old apartment building. Obviously, it *was* an apartment house, but it's been converted into some kind of rooming house. The doors to the rooms are all open. The people inside the rooms are elderly, and they look sick. Some are in bed. Some are sitting by their beds, next to walkers.

Nobody seems surprised to see us going down the hall with our stretcher. Most don't even look up as we go by. It's not a nursing home in the conventional sense. Not like any I've seen. Almost certainly unlicensed. Looks like a home-made nursing home for poor people. A neighborhood co-op nursing home, like a neighborhood garden.

It strikes me that it's kind of nice that something like this exists. The need was there, and somebody made it happen.

The building is clean and the heat is on, even though it's summer. It is cool outside, but it's not that cool. Old sick people are always cold. Somebody cares.

I bet it's a walk-up again. Of course it is. A woman leads us upstairs. She's not wearing a uniform, but she's obviously in charge. It's Sunday. She's the weekend shift. Probably not an RN or even an LPN. Just keeping an eye on things. I suppose she's the one who made the call. Good for her. A lot of looking the other way goes on in places like this.

Up we go, three, four floors. There's a noise, but I can't place it. We're going down the hall in the direction of the room where it's coming from. It sounds like it's coming from an animal being abused in some way. Jesus. Take a deep breath; in we go.

It's difficult to describe what we're seeing; *appalling* seems barely adequate. There is an obese black woman half out of the bed. She's making the animal noises. No words. No screams. Just roars and groans and snarly gurgles. Her eyes are wide open, but I don't think she can see anything. They're darting back and forth really fast. The whites are the color of yellow mustard, and the pupils are dilated all the way. Her head and upper body are wedged between the bed and one of those huge old ornate radiators they call Napoleons. After the pastry or the emperor, I wonder. Have to remember to look that up. This one was full of steam. These are much hotter than the hot-water kind. Burn-you-to-death-hot.

The parts of her head and upper body wedged against the radiator have turned white. The rest is her natural color. No one knows how long she's been like this. Didn't anybody hear the noises. Everyone here is old, so maybe not. She looks pregnant. Pretty sure of that. All her weight seems concentrated in her abdomen. Her limbs look relatively normal in size. She's young enough to be pregnant. I'd say in her late twenties at most. Why is she here with all these old sick people.

Big Al says she isn't pregnant. He says she's in the last stages of cirrhosis, and that's why her abdomen is so distended. Now we're guessing she was near the end when she fell and got stuck between the bed and the radiator and was too weak to get free, so she got slowly cooked.

What a break. Dying from cirrhosis *plus* burned alive by a goddamned radiator.

It's very hard to get her unstuck, and we have to be careful not to get burned ourselves. The Napoleon is still searingly hot, and no one seems to be able to shut it off.

She isn't struggling, but she isn't cooperating, either. She is very heavy, completely inert, and really in there. By the time we get her unstuck and onto the stretcher, she's not making noises anymore. Her eyes are still darting back and forth.

Does she see me. I don't think so. I'm talking to her and telling her it's going to be okay. I tell her we're taking her to the hospital, and she's going to be all right—this being one of our more useful lies. I'm thinking what could she possibly understand at this point. And if she can understand me, is it any comfort. Sometimes, I think it is.

I don't think it matters much this time.

We get her to Elmhurst General, alive, and brief the staff on what we think we've brought them. They don't say anything, but we know they're dismissive of our cirrhosis diagnosis. That's okay with me. I know we're not doctors. We're just telling them what we were told at the scene. They can see the rest of what's happened for themselves. They can see it. Who can say if they believe it.

I wonder if she's going to make it. God forgive me, but I hope she doesn't.

MR. BUBBLE

A CHEVY BEL Air has smashed into a tree on a nice street in Forest Hills. The lone driver is the only casualty. He has submarined under the wheel, and he's stuck in there pretty well. No seat belts in the car. I'm talking to him. He's conscious but very bloody, obviously in a lot of distress but handling the pain well. He's being as tough-guy as his situation allows.

He's a big man. A lot of us say *big* when we really mean hugely fat. *Big,* then, is our standard euphemism for *obese.* So okay, this man is really, really fat. I am thinking that this fatness probably saved his life when he hit the steering wheel.

It doesn't look like he had been going very fast, so we're not expecting extensive internal injuries, but of course it's impossible to tell just by looking. We're wondering how to get him out from under the wheel and onto a stretcher. Luckily, at least in terms of his potential extraction, the seat has slammed up toward the front of the car from the impact, and we're able to release it and slide it back and just ease him out. He insists on walking to the stretcher, which is only a yard or so away. I like this guy.

We get him to St. John's and into the emergency room. In the ER, we do a cut down, scissoring off his clothes to get him ready for treatment and X-rays.

Most of his face and head wounds are bloody but not serious (head wounds always bleed a lot even when they're relatively minor). However, he's having a very hard time breathing now, and he can barely talk. His neck and face are swelling grotesquely. Dr. K. decides something's blocking his trachea, so he plans to make a hole.

Dr. K. is having trouble. He's trying to feel for the trachea with his finger—and his finger is barely up to the task, given the volume of neck fat.

Dr. K. is Dr. Kaplan, a plastic surgeon, doing his required periodic rotation in emergency. I've always thought his fingers were kind of stubby for a surgeon, but he is really talented. I've seen him do some amazing things in the ER and always consider any patient who needs to be sewn up when Dr. K. is on duty to be lucky—relatively speaking.

I think he must take at least eight stitches for every one a *regular* physician makes. More stitches mean smaller scars. I've seen him do mattress sutures so the threads don't go over the wound and give that traditional Frankenstein's monster effect. He's meticulous. I admire him.

Our patient's neck is looking like it belongs on an alpha-male elephant seal. Dr. K. finds his mark, he opens, and in goes the airway. He is so quick. He secures it with adhesive tape, and we roll our patient into the X-ray room.

When they roll him back to the ER twenty minutes later, we all whisper *Holy shit* simultaneously. Is this the same guy. I can't say what his actual percentage increase in size works out to be in numbers, but he's a whole lot bigger than he was when we brought him in. What is going on.

We all look at his X-rays to find an answer, and there it is. Nearly every single one of his ribs, on both sides, is smashed—splintered in *two* places—by the steering wheel. The splintered ribs have shredded his lungs, and the air he would normally be exhaling is staying inside his body instead, inflating him like a balloon.

Every part of his body that offers any available space for inflation is blowing up before our eyes. Dr. K. is palpating the patient's arm. He asks if I want to feel.

What I feel is this: the flesh below the surface of his arm feels like layers of bubbles. The bubbles move around when I squeeze.

Dr. K. tells me what I'm feeling is called crepitus, caused by interstitial emphysema: the spaces in our patient's body are trapping the air pumped from his lungs into, rather than out of, his body.

We're standing by to get the okay to take him upstairs to surgery. This can't wait. It's hard for me to visualize exactly what kind of operation they're going to perform. I don't see how they can repair his lungs, torn to pieces by bone splinters. It occurs to me that they may not know themselves and will just have to see what they can see.

We're all standing around him. Everybody is staring; it's impossible to look away. His scrotum is the size of a small grapefruit and his eyelids look like Ping-Pong balls. They're pressed shut, and he can't see us any longer. He can't see us gawking. His neck is gigantic now, and I'm wondering if it could actually expand to the point where it pulls the airway out of his trachea.

I'm starting to think that now I've seen everything. But, of course, just by virtue of seeing this, I know for a fact that I have not seen, and definitely never will see, everything.

Through it all, this terrific man is trying to reassure or even comfort us. He's patting Dr. K.'s arm, as if to say, Don't worry, it's going to be okay. We get this a lot. Patients often seem to know when they're putting us under stress and try to make *us* feel better. They often apologize to us. This almost always makes us feel worse.

He hasn't lost consciousness and seems pretty stable. All of which would be amazing in any human being, but he is seventy-eight years old.

We get the call to bring him up, and when we leave him, we pat him on the shoulder and say our *good luck*s and go away feeling pretty hopeful. Jesus, can this old hoss absorb the abuse. We're engaged. We're really pulling for him.

They call down from the OR to let us know his heart stopped before they could even get him on the table. It isn't surprising.

But after all he went through and survived, it just doesn't seem fair.

ON A WINE-DARK SEA

SOMEONE HAS GOTTEN me up out of a deep sleep. I'm in the X-ray room on a gurney. It's freezing in here, but it's too hot outside to sleep on the stretcher in the back of the bus. I'm aware that my lower face, from the corner of my mouth to below my chin, is covered with dried drool. I am about eighteen hours into a twenty-four-hour shift, 6:00 a.m. Sunday to 6:00 a.m. Monday, so it must be about 12:00 a.m. Monday morning. We've been going nonstop until around forty-five minutes ago, when I apparently passed out on the gurney.

We have a call. It's a possible DOA in Kew Gardens. We don't go there that much. Fred knows where the address is, though. He knows where everything is. He never seems to need sleep.

I've known Fred since before I started on the job, when I used to pump gas at my father's gas station for the St. John's ambulances and hobnob with the ambulance boys, as Dad called them. Although Fred hardly qualifies as a boy. He seems very old. Not so much in years but in mileage. He's from the Deep South. Way deep. He has a heavy accent. Maybe Mississippi or Alabama. No farther north than that.

Fred is one of those to-the-bone southern guys who grew up with absolutely nothing and will never let himself or the world forget it. But I'd never call him a redneck or a cracker. He's smart as a whip. Skinny as a snake. Mean as a mink. His eyes and cheeks are sunken in, and his nose is huge and hooked. He looks like a large raptor, in profile. Maybe a turkey vulture. Check that. He actually looks like a dead man.

Fred is dead serious about everything and pretty much a drag to be partnered with, but he knows a lot and I feel confident when we're out on a call together. The only time he smiles is when something is bitterly ironic or when he tries to be social and make a joke, which he can't. Maybe he realizes he can't make a joke, and the smile is more of a rueful grimace. He's surprisingly strong, like a lot of these wiry, leathery old southern guys are. My Nashville grandfather was the same way—tough and wiry—but as gentle a man as you'd ever want to meet.

I outweigh Fred by at least fifty pounds, but I wouldn't want to fight him. His *snake is out* and his *11s are up*, which isn't good. The *snake* is what the winos call the blood vessel that becomes prominent on the forehead of someone who's in bad shape; the *11s* are the tendons at the back of the neck that, when wasting is at work, stick out like the number 11. The 11s are considered much worse than the snake, as these things go.

My guess—he's in his late fifties but could be younger. Life has not been kind to Fred, but he'll probably live to be a hundred. These hard, skinny guys are usually the ones who do. Except for the nice ones, like my grandfather.

He's been divorced a long time and lives alone. He doesn't smoke or drink. I'm not sure I've ever seen him eat, which is virtually a team sport with our ambulance gang. I've never been aware of him taking a break for either number one or number two. What he does with his waste is anybody's guess. Is it possible, considering his meager consumption of food and drink, that he actually produces no waste.

So Fred is awake and not talking, and I'm half asleep and incapable of talking, and off we go. No conversation. No lights or sirens, either. There are cops on the scene, and it's not a rush call. They must've woken me up out of a dream on the gurney because it seems like the dream is still in progress.

Here's the house. The patrol car is out front. We go inside.

It's very dark in the house. It seems a lot darker than it should be, even at this wee hour. Here's a little old lady. Who's dead and where are they, I'm wondering and before I can finish the thought, she tells me it's her husband and he's *in there.*

There is a tiny bathroom, barely big enough for the toilet, sink, and tub, which are arranged left to right as I'm looking into the room. What I am seeing is strange and striking. I have to attribute this in part to my extreme fatigue and the fact that many times, very late at night, calls take on a decidedly surreal character that is mesmerizing. But this only looks surreal. It is quite real.

In the middle of this white chamber, on the floor in front of the sink, lies a man curled up in the fetal position. His skin is as white as the porcelain tiles, the sink, and the tub. His pajamas are white. His hair is white. He is lying in an evenly spread aspic of congealed blood. The blood is a gorgeous deep purple red-black. It has a smooth, glossy finish like some sort of fruit glaze on a pastry. There is a four-inch-long clot of dark blood coming out of his nose. This is the entire scene. All white against deep red-black. It's stunning. It's Homer's *wine-dark sea* in forty square feet.

I'm having one of those visual experiences I think they call a trombone shot in the movies. I feel like I'm zooming out and hovering about seven or eight feet above what I'm seeing. This seems to happen a lot on the job, and I can't account for it.

What I also can't account for is why this scene strikes me as beautiful. Of course, it's not beautiful in any conventional sense. It's horrible. A man is dead. He bled out on his bathroom floor. Most likely too much blood thinner plus a major nosebleed.

I'm trying to think what *beautiful* really means. I think most of the time, for most people, it means something good. But I don't think it has to mean good. I've heard the phrase *a terrible beauty,* and I'm thinking, Yes, this is that. It is terrible. And it is beautiful.

And it's unforgettable.

BEER

THERE'S A FULL moon, and Fred and I have been ready for some serious action all night, but it's about 3:00 a.m. and we haven't had any so far. There are supposedly all kinds of statistics about the full moon's effects on humans: more murders, more crime in general, lots of maternities, and so on. But ole Fred don't need no stinking statistics: he knows this is true from firsthand experience.

Yes, it's uncannily quiet out there tonight. Crap. I *would* have to say that—now we're getting a call saying there's a *bleeding psycho* in the basement of an apartment building in Rego Park. What a wonderful, melodramatic term, *psycho.* I wonder which came first—the street slang or the movie. The word itself tells us next to nothing. Other than it's *not* a DOA or maternity or man off a building, and we should be cautious since we have no idea what we're walking into. It could even be dangerous. I'm getting all shivery: a full moon *and* a psycho. Lon Chaney Jr., here we come.

It's a nice building. The call is in the basement, which is apparently an apartment rather than simply a utility area, where the furnace and the laundry equipment are usually located. The door is cracked, and the cops push it open. It's hard, because something is pushing back. Inside is a sea of empty beer cans. Hundreds and hundreds. Maybe thousands. They're at least a foot deep on the floor and rise gradually as they meet the walls, going up at least three feet in places. I think I see the outlines of some furniture under the cans. It looks like a Georgia farm where everything is covered in kudzu.

The smell of sour beer and piss and vomit is overpowering. It's stifling hot in here. There's no damn air. We can't open any windows because we can't get to them for the beer cans.

In the middle of the room, sitting back on a huge mound of empty cans, is a man about fifty years old. He has on a uniform that's covered in puke and blood. One of the cops says he's a beer-truck driver. Oh God, the irony. I allow myself to think this is funny, just for a moment. The beer-truck driver as the little kid with the drink stand who ends up consuming a lot of his inventory himself. I wonder how long this has been going on and if his employer has gotten feedback from customers about their orders being less than complete.

The man's name is Bill. Fred and I chassé our way up to Bill, our feet flat on the floor under the empty cans, sliding smoothly through them to take up positions on either side of him. *Hi, Bill. How are you feeling. Do you want to go to the hospital. Do you think you can stand up.* He nods yes and yes and tries to say something but can only make gurgling sounds. His mouth is full of blood; it's coming out the sides when he tries to talk. He's bleeding a lot. Bleeding ulcers perhaps. That's my bet, given the huge quantities of beer he must consume on a regular basis.

His pulse is still okay, and he's alert and looking at us when we speak to him, but that won't be the case for long with this much bleeding, so we have to get moving. Anyway, judging by his alertness, Bill is no psycho.

Whoever made the call probably hadn't seen him for a while. Maybe he didn't show up for work, and his boss called the landlord, and the landlord knocked and only heard gurgling and thought Bill was going nuts. The call probably came in like: I have this tenant and can't get in his unit and he's making these animal kind of noises and I'm afraid he's crazy or something...Direct translation from Central to St. John's 433: *Psycho.*

Bill, can you stand up for us. That's good. *Do you think you can walk with us to the ambulance outside.* Great. It's not that we're lazy. This is just more efficient. We could go back through the cans, down the sidewalk, open the doors, and pull out the stretcher, then make our way back, but it's a time waster, and Bill is nodding and gurgling, *Yes, I can make it,* so off we go.

All the way I'm asking him what happened, and it seems like he's really trying to tell me, but I can't understand a word of it, and neither can Fred.

We help him up into the ambulance, but he clearly doesn't want to lie back and would rather sit up on the stretcher, which is reasonable, given that he would almost surely choke on his own blood if he were to lie down. I look under the bench seat and bring out a handful of plastic bags, because he's bleeding that bad.

We love these plastic bags. When patients vomit or bleed orally, these bags are a must. We buy them ourselves because the equipment they give us for this, the intolerably cutely named *emesis basins,* is absurd. These stainless-steel basins are the kidney-shaped bowls you see when your doctor gives you a shot and needs a little container to put the gauze and syringe in or whatever. They're really small and hard to grip and, worst of all, they catch and hold almost nothing. Ambulance-worthy patients who vomit almost always do so in large volumes, and to see it come blasting out in a moving ambulance and hit the rounded sides of the dainty basin and carom off onto the stretcher and the floor of the bus and your uniform and arms and face is not any fun at all. The plastic bags hold a lot, and you can tie them off.

Bill, see if you can hold this for me. He can. The bag is filling up as I get out my pen and pink sheet on its little clipboard and try to get some information. We're moving fast.

Full lights and siren. I have learned to write pretty well in a bouncing, lurching ambulance. The downside is I seem to be losing the ability to write legibly when I'm sitting still. Fred radios Central and tells them we're 10-20 to Elmhurst General with a rush bleeder and they should be ready for us. Amazing. From psycho to rush bleeder in the blink of an eye. You just never know.

Bill still can't talk. His bag is half full, and I hand him another. He's trying to tell me something, over and over again. It has a speechlike cadence to it and almost makes sense. It sounds like *Ah ankh ayno*. Sounds vaguely Egyptian. It must be the *ankh* part. He's clearly frustrated that he can't get it across. For sure no psycho. Not even drunk, although I don't see how that's possible, given all the empty beer cans.

Bag number 2 is ready to tie off, and I place it carefully next to the first and hand him a third. We're at an impasse. He's still trying to tell me what's wrong. I still can't understand him. He's still bleeding. I wonder how many bags he can go through before they're all full and he's empty.

I think we may have a breakthrough. There is an *aha* light in Bill's eyes, and he starts pointing at me. It scares me for an instant. It feels like some kind of accusation or warning. Oh. He's not pointing at me; he's pointing at my pen and the pink call slip on my clipboard. He trades me his bag for my pen and paper, and he immediately writes: *I drank Drano.* Oh shit.

Shit, shit, *shit.*

I look at his words, and then I look at him, and just to make sure I'm reading this right, I shout (Fred is standing on the siren and it's deafening), *You drank Drano,* and Bill nods very slowly. He looks like a kid who has just confessed to breaking a prized knickknack. He's ashamed.

I hand him back his bag, and he continues his bleeding. I put my pen in my pocket to concentrate on doing whatever I can for the man, which is pretty much nothing. He can't lie down, so all I can do is steady him as we jounce along and have more bags ready. All the while I'm wondering how this happened.

Was he in a stupor with an upset stomach and thought he was taking Bromo-Seltzer or something like that. Was he trying to kill himself. He could have picked a better way. When I say *better,* I don't mean more effective, just quicker or less painful. I know that most would-be suicides who survive a jump tell of regretting it on the trip down. If suicide was Bill's plan, I imagine he's regretting it now.

I am thinking about what is happening inside of Bill. Drano is a strong base and just as caustic as a strong acid. It is burning through Bill's flesh and disintegrating his capillaries as it makes its way through his digestive tract. The capillaries in his mouth and throat, his esophagus and stomach. This kind of bleeding isn't like arterial bleeding, where you can apply pressure and stop it or at least slow it down until it can be tied off. What's to press. This is why wounds to the stomach or liver are so tricky. They're full of capillaries and it's so hard to stop the bleeding. I think most people picture bleeding to death as blood spurting dramatically out of an artery. *Bleeding out.* But *oozing out* is just as effective, if less flamboyant. Then there are the chemical burns to the other tissues. I'm trying to picture how much of Bill's esophagus is left when we pull into EGH. Poor Bill.

There are a lot of personnel, an unusually high number, in the ER when we roll in. Must be the full-moon contingent.

We get Bill into a wheelchair and roll him in, bag in hand. We step back quickly because Bill is immediately swarmed by a cordon of residents, interns, and doctors of every stripe. Word that we were on the way with a Drano case seems to have drawn every available MD from whatever he or she was doing to see it. What they are going to do for Bill is anybody's guess. *My* guess is: nothing.

Tonight I had plans to go out with my friend Gary and have a few beers. I think I'm going to pass.

BREAKFAST OF CHAMPIONS

CENTRAL SAYS WE have a female DIB (difficulty in breathing) and put a rush on it. We're off. No need for the lights or siren. There's almost nobody on the road. It's about 5:00 a.m., and most New Yorkers sleep late on Sunday. We've been on since 6:00 a.m. yesterday, almost finished with a twenty-four-hour shift.

I'm on with Andy Panda (he hates that nickname, and I never use it to his face, obviously), and we've had a hearty breakfast—egg sandwiches, the wonderful kind with the yolk that spurts out when you bite down, and hash browns and doughnuts and Danish and two coffees and juice. We bought a *New York Times* to share. One of us will take over the puzzle when the other one gets stuck. In the unlikely event that one of us finishes the whole puzzle, we'll buy another *Times.*

Andy's one of my favorites. He's a big guy, like a big teddy—or panda—bear. Baby faced. Like a big kid. He lives with his mum—he really calls her that. They emigrated from England when he was just a nipper. No mention of his father, and I've never asked. One time we stopped by their apartment, and I met his mother and he showed me their prized possession: an ornate helmet they claimed came from the Light Brigade. I didn't see any cannon-shrapnel holes. It looked really new and was well polished—like something the kaiser would have worn to inspect his troops. I was skeptical, I have to admit. But I did my best to appear appropriately appreciative.

Andy never went to college, but he's exceptionally well read. Plus, he's naturally smart, which helps him take his reading and turn it into understanding. That, combined with the street smarts you get on a job like this, makes for a very tolerable twenty-four-hour-shift companion. He definitely knows his shit as far as emergencies are concerned. He's not that much older than I am, at nineteen, but he seems older and wiser, and I tend to think of him as kind of a big brother.

Andy works two jobs. Several of the St. John's guys do. This is one reason the night shift is so popular—it gives them time for another gig. Some of them make pretty big bucks for blue-collar guys—but that's always been true of NYC: if you want to bust your hump, you can make some serious cash. I can make tuition for a year at Vanderbilt working for St. John's in a single summer. It's good money. But I'd never have the energy to take another job in addition to this one. I don't know when those guys sleep, but they seem healthy and alert enough. Mazel tov, boys. Better you than me.

Andy's other job is driving the truck that collects corpses from the city morgues and delivers them to the potter's field on Hart Island. This is one of those jobs you wouldn't dream existed unless somebody told you about it. And if you did know about it, you'd never figure out what you had to do to get it. There's a whole parallel reality of jobs like this in a city like New York. Hidden jobs. Jobs that almost no one is aware of as they go about their day-to-days.

Dad has a guy named Steve who opens up the gas station every morning at six. When I was little, Dad told me the reason Steve got there so early was because he was coming from his other job, which was turning off all the streetlights in the city. This fascinated me until I realized that, like Santa visiting every rooftop in the world, it was absurd. But when I think of Andy's morgue job and others like it, I think of Steve and the streetlights and wonder how many other strange and secret New York jobs that might seem absurd are, in fact, real.

Andy's morgue job is dead simple. Pick up the van—it looks like a bread truck—and then make the rounds. I've seen these trucks from the outside. They're custom fitted, with multiple coffin racks installed for the un-claimed dead. That's who goes to the potter's field—the unclaimed. Some of them have not been identified. Some have been identified, but there's no one to notify, to claim them for burial. Some of them belong to people who have been notified but have no money for a burial. And some of them belong to people who have been notified but couldn't care less.

New arrivals are buried three deep and carefully cataloged for possible reburial if someone should eventually show up to claim them. If not, Andy tells me, they wait six years, and if no one has shown up, they exhume what's left and dump the remains out at sea. I have no way of verifying this. I guess I will have to file this with the helmet from the Light Brigade: *Hold for verification.*

He says he has seen some pretty awful things on his morgue job. The one that sticks in my mind is his description of a morgue attendant jumping up and down on a body to get it into one of the pine boxes they use as coffins. This I can believe. These boxes are impossibly narrow. I've seen them and I can't see how anybody fits. So I could understand how they might have to use a bit of force to get a body into one, since it's definitely not a one-size-fits-all proposition. Rigor mortis is not a consideration—it's usually gone in a couple of days, and the unclaimed bodies are in the morgue at least that long before they're boxed up. They are embalmed before burial, but they're kept at only around thirty-four degrees Fahrenheit before that. I suppose if they froze them it would damage tissues and prevent an accurate autopsy.

The fact that they're not frozen means they make the whole place stink. When I see a movie or television show where a jolly ME is sitting in the morgue munching on a sandwich, it's really irritating. It would make me want to throw up.

I had a hair-trigger gag reflex growing up. I got carsick almost every time I got in a car. I couldn't eat pasta with tomato sauce for several years, to the great amusement of my father's side of the family. The Italians. Even colors, one in particular, set my gorge to rising: a pastel aqua-green. A color found on certain Fords of the day as well as some flavors of saltwater taffy. Considering the truly awful smells we encounter on the ambulance—decomposition, gangrene, gastrointestinal bleeding—I'm amazed I've never hurled. Visual stuff like carnage, blood, gore, and the like have little effect on me, at least hurl-wise.

Here we are. Let's meet our rush female DIB. Well, bless her heart—it's a sweet little old lady. She's conscious, and her color is good. Her pulse is okay. I don't think she weighs more than seventy pounds. She's communicative. *Hello, Mother.* (I've picked this greeting up from the other guys when we have a call with a patient like this. They seem to love it.) She's having moderate difficulty breathing but nothing that seems immediately life threatening. We lift her onto the stretcher—she's as light as a marshmallow—and roll her outside and into the ambulance.

We're under way. Now she seems to be having more

trouble. I raise the back of the stretcher a bit higher and start giving her oxygen. The mask is over her mouth and nose. *Are you comfortable. Is that too tight,* I ask as we bounce up Queens Boulevard. She wants to tell me something. She's insistent.

I take the mask down and lean in close to ask her what she has to say. I am in midsentence when she vomits directly into my open mouth.

I, in turn, immediately encase her in generous amounts of egesta composed almost completely of the huge breakfast I have consumed not twenty-five minutes prior to this very moment. Some of the ingredients are still quite recognizable. She, however, is not.

Her entire head and shoulders are obscured with the remains of my morning meal. I'm horrified. *Mortified.* As I stare at her unrecognizable form, I can see movement. Two apertures open up in the mass that is covering her face, and I see her shiny blue eyes looking at me through the vomit. She is blinking slowly. Her mouth is open, but she isn't saying anything. Interestingly, she no longer seems to be having any difficulty breathing. Have I shocked her into wellness.

I look up and see Andy's eyes in the rearview mirror. Total shock is an understatement.

We're pulling into St. John's. I see the looks on the faces of the staff as we roll our patient into the ER and transfer her to a gurney. They don't have to ask what happened.

They can see that. Maybe later, they'll ask how. Right now, they're as stupefied as our patient, Andy, and I.

So much for my perfect no-hurl record as an attendant on St. John's Queens ambulance. I suppose, like any record, it was meant to be broken. In rather extravagant fashion, at that. Andy says I'd better change my shirt and rinse my mouth out while I'm at it. I told you he was smart.

BOUDICCA GOES SOFT

IT'S A NICE, quiet Sunday morning, and I'm at my *command center* in the ER. It's a desk with a phone behind a high counter, where I can sit to take calls and relax when we're between runs. There's another room to the side of this where some of the other guys regularly congregate to read the paper, eat, or just bullshit. Usually we're all outside, and someone who's covering the phone will come out with the call. But when it's hot or when we're noshing, we like to be inside with the AC.

The ER is small, with seats for about twenty people. Even though it's quiet for us on the ambulance today, the ER seats are almost filled to capacity, with mostly trivial injuries like minor burns, scrapes—really nonemergencies. Most people don't have the faintest concept of ordinary first aid and so come here to get their boo-boos kissed, figuratively speaking. We also have a regular Sunday-morning contingent that comes in for B_{12} shots. I'm told most of them are alcoholics getting these shots as a kind of tonic—it seems to make them feel better, but I think that's largely a placebo effect. Whatever works.

The nurse in charge today is a force of nature. Boudicca in white. It is simply not possible to be more Irish-Catholic-Celtic than she is. If I were going to cast her part in a hospital-ER movie, the role could be played only by Maureen O'Hara. *Hard as nails* is an accurate but inadequate cliché to describe this nurse, whom I shall call Pegeen because I'm actually afraid of what she might do if she sees I had the sand to use her real name. I think *Pegeen* is Irish enough to do the job. She's in her late forties, I guess. Around six feet in her white nurse stockings. Maybe taller than that. And big boned.

She's always giving me shit, in the way of a cantankerous longshoreman. If we bring in a bad one, she gives us that banshee look, the Irish stink eye. It makes me feel that if she had a ruler on her, she'd smack us across the knuckles, or worse.

Once, when I had finished a shift, I walked up Fifty-Seventh Avenue to my father's gas station to meet him there so we could ride home together. My cousin George was there with his new used bike. It had drop handlebars, which, for reasons only known to him, he had turned up—so that he could sit more upright, I suppose. The result of this modification was to place the brake levers in a position where they could only be actuated by leaning back and using your thumbs. He asked me if I wanted to take it for a spin. I hopped on.

I had not gone a block when I reached an intersection. A car was coming on my right. In an instant, I could see he didn't see me. Apparently, he didn't see the stop sign, either. I instinctively reached for the brakes, which of course weren't where they were supposed to be. I knew he was going to hit me. I tried to relax. The impact slammed the bike out from under me. I slid up the length of the hood to the windshield, smacked into that, and was launched high into the air, clear across the intersection. To my great amazement, I landed on my feet, shoeless. My canvas boat shoes, still perfectly tied, lay under the bike, just as if I had pushed them off and left them there, side by side. I have seen this quite a few times on the ambulance and always wondered how it happens—what's the science. I know about inertia, but it's hard for me to believe the impact could have forced me out of those lightweight shoes. Anyway, it happens, and now it has happened to me.

I was okay except that my wrist had gotten whacked by the insanely positioned brake lever when the handlebars were twisted out of my hands from the impact. I duly walked what was left of the bike back to George and then started down the street to St. John's.

Pegeen was there to greet me with scorn that was exceptionally keen, even for her. I told her what had happened. I thought my wrist might be broken, and she said if it were, she'd eat her hat. When the X-ray showed it was chipped and I demanded she eat her hat, I actually thought she was going to belt me one.

That's our Boudicca. Hard, cynical, and Celtic to the core. But it's quiet today and I'm absorbed in the crossword and Pegeen is out of sight in the OR, treating patients.

I'm gradually becoming aware of a stir in the ER. A rustle of murmurs is passing through the waiting patients and their escorts. They're staring toward the double doors that lead into the ER. There's a man standing very still, looking around, clearly dazed and very feeble. He's dressed in filthy rags.

Under these rags, every square inch of him is completely covered with thick, caked-on shit. It's as if he's been iced by some demented baker.

We're all staring at him in silent shock. God, he stinks so bad—and I am no stranger to stink. I can't imagine what the patients must think. I'm wondering how dried feces could smell so bad—shouldn't they be more or less descented by the time they turn into adobe. He must have been shitting himself for weeks. Maybe months. How the hell did it get up to his neck and his head and in his hair—was he pooping upside down.

Everyone in the room is frozen. The guy is frozen. I'm trying to decide if I should press the buzzer to alert security. If I do, what will I say. What kind of an incident is this.

The doors to the OR are opening. It's Pegeen. Her sixth

sense and the quiet in the ER must have told her something was up—she really doesn't miss a thing. She immediately zeroes in on our visitor. I have never seen her face like this.

Imagine the Virgin Mary with a new puppy, and you will begin to visualize the look of benignity on the feral Pegeen's face.

Talk about your angels of mercy—I'm looking at one right now. Who *is* this person. All eyes have shifted from shit man to her as she walks toward him, her expression never changing, and takes him by the filth-covered arm. She's speaking to him in a low voice, sounding so sweet; noises like you make when you talk to a baby or a kitten or a loved one or someone who's dying. Where is she taking him. She's asking me to come with and, of course, I do. Everyone always does what she tells them, even though this time she's asking, not telling. I'm transfixed and completely in her power.

There's an area where we never go, adjacent to the ER. It's a cozy bedroom reserved for the doctor on call, seriously off-limits to anyone else. In it, there is a large walk-in shower. Pegeen is leading this man to the stall. Holy Christ. She's going to give him a shower. She's turning on the shower, but she's not tossing him in. She's not asking me to do a thing. Am I here to help, or simply stand guard.

Maybe she just wants someone to know who she really is.

Instead of putting him in the shower fully dressed, which would make sense, she's removing his clothing. It is beyond disgusting, but she's not wearing gloves. She is gingerly—make that *tenderly*—taking off his garments and dropping them on the floor of the shower. I'm trying to observe without staring. I don't want to violate what little self-esteem the man has left.

Pegeen is filling a basin with shower water and squirting in some pHisoHex. Now she has a sponge and she's soaking it in the soapy water. She's going in to wash the man by hand, as if he were a baby.

We've all seen the paintings of Christ's body being cleaned for burial. This is like that. It is a moment of such impossible charity and tenderness that it has brought me to the verge of tears. I cannot allow her to see me cry. I'd never live it down. She'd see to that. I'm out of here.

The next time we see this man, he looks brand-new. He's clean and wearing newly laundered surgical scrubs and disposable slippers. Even his hair is combed.

It's almost impossible to believe, but Pegeen's starched white nurse's vestments are completely spotless. It's like a miracle.

Boudicca turns and shoots me a fierce look that tells me I'd better keep my mouth shut if I know what's good for me.

I do, and I do.

DEATH OF A CYNIC

I LOVE WEDDINGS, and this one seems better than the usual. For one thing, it's a nice hall, not too schmaltzy. My sisters (two out of three) are obsessed about having their reception at Leonard's of Great Neck, having been there for a couple of dos and having seen the gilded extravagances (my view) first-hand. They'll have to wait, since they're fourteen and ten right now. Sister number 3 is a toddler, so she has yet to weigh in on the subject. They're all here somewhere, I assume with Mom and Dad or some cousins, or sitting at the bar having Shirley Temples. They love to sit at the bar. We call them bar fleas, in light of their tender years. This is a cousin wedding. Cousin Ralph. He's my favorite cousin. We spent a lot of time hanging out as small kids, and I'm happy to be here.

I've had more than a few drinks, but I'm doing okay. In New York, the drinking age is eighteen, which means we've all been drinking since a few years before that. So it isn't hitting me like a ton of lead. I'm in a second- or third-tier crowd—no one seems to have any clear relationship to the principals: the lucky couple, their parents, whoever. I think one of these invitees works with someone who's related to someone who works with the bride. What that makes him is anybody's guess.

We're all talking about what we do. For a living, school, what. My turn finally comes, and I start telling them that I work for St. John's (which is literally a mile down Queens Boulevard from where we are right now) on the ambulance, and the one who's related to someone immediately zooms in on what I'm saying.

He's telling me that a couple of months ago his mother was in an accident on Queens Boulevard and she was picked up by St. John's ambulance and taken to the hospital, where she was admitted for a severely broken neck. It's a miracle she wasn't paralyzed, and so forth. This is very interesting to me. When did this happen, where, what time of day, I ask. He describes a call that I remember very well, having been half of the team that responded.

I am overcome by a tremendous shock. It feels the way you feel when you've come close to serious harm, like almost stepping back off the edge of a very high place. The adrenaline rush is palpable. My heart is pounding, and it isn't from the ethanol. Yes, I remember this call *exceptionally* clearly.

We're living in the age of a medical (and legal) phenomenon called whiplash. I'm not sure the word even existed before a year or so ago, outside of pirate ships or torture chambers. Not in the context in which it's being used today, at any rate.

People in NYC get really smart really fast, especially

when there's a buck in it. It became known by millions, al-most overnight, that a small bump on the back of your car could have dollar signs attached. Accidents that for years went unreported were suddenly being backed up with le-gal briefs that could choke a horse. Everyone—anyone, driver or passengers—could file a claim for whiplash if the car they were riding in was hit from behind. I'm sure huge numbers of claims were filed even when the claimants weren't hit from behind—fault is almost always assigned to whoever hits you, anywhere but the very front of your car. The sides and rear are whiplash territory.

Overnight, simple sprained necks were turning into a cash bonanza for the car-riding public at large, not to men-tion the legal and medical professions. It's no exaggeration to say that nearly every accident we respond to, not count-ing those where the victims are truly injured or dead, in-volves the word *whiplash*. Neck pain is always noted on our pink call slips. These slips are official documents, and I sup-pose they can be subpoenaed as evidence in a whiplash lawsuit, even though most of these suits are pretty pro forma. The claimant wears a neck brace for a while. The ac-tion is filed. The money is paid. The neck brace goes into the garbage. Or it's reserved for another family member. *Waste not, want not,* as the saying goes.

The woman we picked up on Queens Boulevard that day, the only person claiming injury in the accident, was com-plaining about her neck. She didn't have to say the w-word;

I knew where this was heading. That day, I was working with a guy about my age. I think he is from one of the *-stan*s in central Asia. He has a very slight accent, and his name is Richie. I try to imagine what his *-stan* name is, but for the life of me, I can't back out of *Richie* into anything that makes sense. I'll have to ask him someday. Richie is in medical school. He has finished his first year and done well. Richie is affable, not too serious, and very smart. I like working with him, but I don't have a chance to often, which is too bad.

I was just about to take Richie aside and lay *Yet another frigging whiplash* on him when a strange look came over his face. Not *weird* strange, just serious, which was strange for him. He was worried about her neck, he said. *Let's put on a neck splint*, he said. *A what*, I said. You're shitting me, I thought. I must have been dozing off when they taught neck splints. Never heard of one. Never saw one. I've seen those orthopedic neck braces but never a *splint*, per se. As far as I knew, we didn't have any under the bench or below the floor in the ambulance, where we keep all our stuff.

Richie, we don't have any neck splints, do we, I asked. Richie didn't skip a beat: *We're going to make one.* I had been a Boy Scout and knew how to improvise all kinds of things, from emergency shelters to rope bridges to drinking cups from tree bark. Richie's plan intrigued me. He started rummaging under the bench and came up with two stretcher sheets and a wide roll of adhesive tape. He was very methodical, moving slowly. Or he only seemed slow, in contrast to the speed at which traffic was passing us on either side of the ambulance. People rarely slow down for accidents. You have to be very deliberate in your movements when you're working around an ambulance, treating people out in the street. If not, you could end up needing treatment yourself. It happens often enough.

Richie decided he only needed one sheet after all. He folded that one a couple of times and rolled it up tight. Then we went over to our patient, who had been very nice while we were making our preparations. Richie had me carefully raise the woman's head and shoulders together as he eased the roll under and around her neck so that both ends of the roll were even in front. He then began to bind the rolled ends together with adhesive tape. The result was what they call a horse collar. (This I found out later, in the course of my remedial neck-splint research.) It did the job perfectly—immobilizing the neck—and I complimented Richie, although he didn't seem to hear me.

We lifted her gently into the ambulance and took her to St. John's.

This was the mother who could have been paralyzed because I allowed myself to be cynical about whiplash and almost didn't take her seriously. The very mother whose actual son is now thanking me profusely to my face for the care I gave her that afternoon on Queens Boulevard. Oh man.

Thank God for Richie.

Who cares what his real name is.

A DATE FOR THE PROM

IT'S AROUND LUNCHTIME on a Tuesday, and we're on the way to another *psycho*. It's our third one today. I can't understand it. There's no full moon. Sometimes you get similar kinds of calls bunched up like this, and then you don't get any for a long while.

One week it seemed like every other fender bender we went to ended up being a major conflagration. There must have been something in the atmospheric conditions that made them burn so easily. We're talking fatalities where there normally would have been cuts and bruises. Another time, we had three stabbings in a row, in the space of an afternoon.

I'm out with Jose today. Jose is from Peru, and he looks exactly as if he has been reanimated from a pre-Columbian pictograph carved on the side of an Aztec or a Mayan temple. He has a wonderful native Mesoamerican profile, and it's really striking. He's shorter than I am, and I'm not tall by any means. I'd say he's about five foot three or so. He is barrel chested and, like all the other guys I work with, really strong—and not just *for his size*. He's nothing, if not cheerful. He's actually funny as hell. In fact, he's a bona-fide pisser.

Jose likes girls a lot. He has a repertoire of appreciative noises that he uses when he sees a woman he admires, which includes just about everyone with two X chromosomes. These noises include: a rapid inhalation of breath (like the sound you'd make if you had just burned yourself on a hot stove), a kissy noise, and a kissy noise combined with a clicky noise combined with a grunt.

Jose has a catalog of gestures as well, which are more or less universal in meaning.

In fairness to Jose, I need to say that none of these noises or gestures is ever directed toward patients, nor are they apparent to the public, since they are almost always expressed inside the ambulance, clearly for my benefit—in reference to individuals he sees on the street.

Jose is the most energetic guy I work with, by a good margin. He literally never stops moving or talking (when he isn't making mating calls), and he kind of wears me out, funny as he is. When he does quiet down, all he has to do is make a face to get me laughing uncontrollably. That wears me out even further. A shift with Jose is like being at a kid's birthday party with an overcaffeinated clown. Stimulating, but you can't wait for it to be over. On the plus side, he helps me practice my Spanish, and we sometimes spend the greater part of a shift speaking in that language only.

We arrive at a very nice building in Forest Hills. Quite fancy. There's a cop waiting to take us upstairs. The apartment is as nice as the building we're in, which isn't always the case. There's another cop here and three other people: Mom, Dad, and a little girl about seven or eight years old. So who's the psycho.

It turns out that Mom and Dad have documents for their daughter that will admit her for psych treatment (or internment) in an appropriate facility, which in this case is Elmhurst General Hospital—St. John's doesn't have a psych ward. The only other place we take psych patients besides EGH, and rarely at that, is the forbidding G Building at Kings County.

None of these facilities is a long-term psych hospital. The long-term places I know of are Creedmoor in Queens Village and (make the Sign of the Cross when you say this) Pilgrim State, out in Brentwood. Grim and grimmer.

This little girl is a lamb. Goldilocks. Alice in Wonderland. The whole call has me puzzled. You don't call an ambulance over a kid like this. You call when someone's possibly violent to themselves or to others or causing a major disturbance. It may be that we have a Dr. Jekyll and Miss Hyde here, but it sure doesn't look like it. Maybe the parents don't drive or don't have a car. But seriously, we're not a taxi service. We're kind of in a gray area right now.

We could legally refuse this call. Of course, we won't. That would be, I don't know…rude, to say the least. Or even immoral. These people seem so nice. Then again the little girl reminds me of one of my sisters, who is perfectly *normal,* whatever that is, but acts much crazier than this little girl is behaving. I'm starting to feel really sad about this call. How could such a sweet kid be mentally ill enough to have to be taken to the hospital—in an ambulance, no less. It's hard to believe. I mean, I don't *want* to believe it.

Hi, dear. How are you today. Do you want to come for a ride with us. Mom and Dad can come, too. Everyone is all smiles except the girl, whose name is Lilly. Lilly's face turns from a pleasant smile to a blank stare to a pout to a frown. Well, surprise, surprise: she doesn't want to go.

I don't think there's going to be a struggle, and I'm reasonably sure the four of us, Jose, the cops, and I, could take her in a fair fight. We outweigh her by at least seven hundred pounds, give or take. What we have here is a standoff. We're all cajoling her the best way we know how. Mom, Dad, the cops, Jose, and I are using our best coaxing skills, but they're not working. She starts smiling again, and we think we may be on the verge of a breakthrough. But we're not. The smile is inappropriate. It's a little unsettling. It's probably good that they called us.

We look at Mom and Dad. They look at each other. The cops look at Jose and me as if we're going to pull some kind of solution out of a hat, being the *experts* on the scene. In the middle of this unspoken game of *what do you want to do/I don't know what do you want to do,* I'm aware that Lilly is smiling at *me.* Really beaming. It's one of the more beatific smiles I've ever seen, and it takes me completely aback. She's whispering something, and we all crane forward to hear. She says, *You're cute.* To me. I am stunned and more than a little embarrassed. Jose makes a low air-sucky sound and elbows me in the ribs.

Mom and Dad are smiling and I am, too, because now I have an idea. First of all, I thank Lilly for her compliment. Then: *Do you want to go to the prom with me, Lilly. I'm going there now. Do you want to come.*

Lilly lights up instantly. *Yes.* Eureka. We're in business. I turn sideways and present her with my arm. She knows just what to do and she takes it, like we've been going steady for years. Out the apartment door we go, into the elevator, trailing a coterie of parents, police, and Jose.

Lilly and I, the king and the queen of the prom.

We're going down the steps from the lobby to the ambulance when I hear a hoarse sound. It's very close, and I start to look around but immediately realize it has come from me: a convulsive gasp of breath; the prelude to a sob. I hope no one has noticed, but they must have heard. All the way to Elmhurst General, everyone is very quiet. No one says a thing.

Not even Jose.

THE WHIRLPOOL

I KNOW WHERE we are. I've been here before. This is the start of my second year on the ambulance, and already I can remember individual calls, where and what and who they were. And God, do I remember this one. I haven't been able to forget it a single day since. Or night.

His name is still on the little black-and-white Dymo label by his door buzzer. All caps. I assume they never relet his apartment. At least they could have peeled his label off. Is this supposed to be some kind of cheesy memorial or a subtle reminder to the other tenants not to let *that* happen again.

I don't think they need a message to remind them of what happened here. These people certainly remember. All these people crowded in this elderly woman's apartment exactly one floor above his apartment. Just exactly above it.

We got this call as a DIB, difficulty in breathing. The woman is sitting up and not in too much distress. Maybe she could breathe a little easier if the throng of neighbors hovering around her would back off a few feet, thank you. This is turning out to be a pretty routine call. I bring up the stretcher, and we settle her in for the trip to St. John's. I'm giving her oxygen while I'm thinking about my last trip to this building in Forest Hills, one floor below.

I was on with Felix, aka the Cat. It was only my second or third week on the ambulance. I had already been on a lot of calls, many of them with Felix. I don't like working with Felix because he's so overbearing, but I think my judgment was prejudiced by this particular call.

It was a miserably hot day in early summer. An early Sunday morning. We got a call, possible DOA in Forest Hills. First call of the day.

I hadn't been to this area on a call before. We don't get a lot of calls in Forest Hills, especially this far south. Felix knew just where it was, though, and had no trouble finding it. We pulled up in front of a substantial dark brick apartment building, maybe eight stories high. Nothing struck me as out of the ordinary until we stepped into the vestibule where the mailboxes were.

The odor was unlike anything I had ever smelled before. It was incredibly foul, and the heat didn't help. It was a complicated smell. Like shit mixed with ammonia and natural gas from a stove and rotten meat and vomit all rolled up into one. And it was starting to make me feel sick.

I felt even sicker when they told us the call was on the

sixth floor. The *sixth* floor. And it smelled that bad down in the lobby.

Felix had a strange look on his face, like a mask. He didn't say anything all the way up in the elevator. At least he wasn't busting my chops. Thank God for small favors. We were ascending with the super, who looked extremely upset. The elevator stank inside.

When he opened the elevator door, the stench just about knocked us over. It was almost unbearably intense. There were two cops on the floor, all the way down the hall, by an open casement window, talking quietly.

When we stepped into the hall, they just looked our way and stared, without saying anything. What the hell was this.

Nobody knew yet. Felix and I were standing in front of an apartment door. No one had been inside so far. No one was sure what was in there, but we all had a good idea. I was getting light-headed from the smell and the heat in the hallway.

There was something dead in there. It *could* have been an animal or two, I reminded myself—some dogs someone left behind and never came back to get. Maybe the tenants went out and got killed in a car crash. Maybe they went on vacation. Maybe they skipped town one step ahead of the law and left the pets to starve to death and rot. Maybe a lot of things. Any one of these scenarios has happened many times, I'd been told. As much as I love animals, I hoped it was one of these scenarios.

Apparently nobody had seen the tenant for quite a while. It looked like we were about to see him now.

All eyes were on the super as he turned his passkey in the lock. Neither of the cops budged from his post by the open window. Felix stepped back, behind me. It was Mr. Super, me, and Felix. That was the lineup. With Cop 1 and Cop 2 in reserve. The super pushed the door open slowly.

A stifling, humid, palpable wave of stench punched us in the face, causing us to simultaneously whip our heads to the side to avoid inhaling it. It was too late. It was in our noses and on our clothes and in our mouths. It must have been more than a hundred degrees in the apartment; it was in the nineties outside. Whatever was in there had been festering but good. And then I saw what it was.

About eight or nine feet away there was a large mass, which used to be a human being, on its side on the floor in front of a couch. The room was full of flies. I mean *full*. Thousands. Felix asked the super to get a couple of bottles of ammonia to smash against the walls so we could run in and open the windows and the flies would be able to escape.

I wondered if this would work. I wondered if he had ever done this before. But my wondering was pointless. The super was out of service, standing to the side of the door vomiting in the hall. He wasn't going anywhere, much less on an errand to fetch ammonia. The cops still hadn't moved an inch. Well, I could sure see why. They'd been down this street before; I was certain.

Seeing the super throwing up, I used all my strength not to do the same. Actually, it wouldn't have mattered if he had been vomiting. I was just about there anyway. It's a reflex, and I was determined to fight it. Standing there trying to stay composed, I felt a poke in the back. It was Felix the Cat. I turned to see what he wanted.

Go ahead in there, kid, and take a good look—you're going to have to get used to it were his exact words.

Maybe if I had been on the job a little while longer and was a little surer of myself, I would have told him to get screwed and stood my ground outside the apartment. But I was a newbie. And I was confused and disoriented. It was as if all my synapses were firing at once. I walked into the room and stood over the rotting body. Right over him. Felix never set one foot inside the apartment.

The smell was so intense that I had two fingers jammed up my nose as far as they would go, but it did no good. I could still smell it. Nothing could block it out. I could taste it clearly. The air was thick with the smell. It had substance. Air is a fluid, just like water. Air has density. I was drinking the air.

As I looked down at the remains, it seemed like I was very tall and able to take in everything in the room all at once in a wide-angle view while still being able to go macro on the details. The details. The gory details, as they say.

This man, or what had been a man, was dressed in a

sleeveless T-shirt and boxers. It looked like he may have been lying on the couch and somehow ended up on the floor, on his left side, just in front of it. I say on his left side—he had no left side. What had been his left side had grown into the carpet. Just coalesced with the carpet. It was as if he had melted into the carpet, and he and the carpet were all one piece.

Where his hair ought to have been, there appeared to be long gray-and-white filaments of mold.

Instead of a face, there was a flat, oval plane covered with maggots. No sign of a nose. Just one wet, gray surface with its seething, ivory-colored veneer of larvae.

His shoulder was the yellow color of parchment and looked translucent. His legs appeared stuck together and were the color of light terra-cotta with a darker maroon line between them, where they were attached. His feet were bare, and his toes were splayed apart grotesquely.

There were globs of black matter on the walls and the ceiling. I had been told that decomposing corpses could generate enormous amounts of gas and could actually burst if the gas couldn't get out naturally. This gas is generated by bacteria that are always present in our bodies. Waiting for the chance to have the last laugh, I suppose. Normally, the skin would gently rupture anyway and let the gases out. Or the gas would pass out of the mouth and anus. I know that late at night, in the morgue, when it's very quiet, you can hear the bodies fart. But the release can sometimes be dramatic. It was dramatic enough here to leave flesh all over the apartment.

My mind was in total overload. This man had been somebody's baby. Cradled in someone's arms. He could have had a girlfriend who passed him notes in fourth grade. Maybe he had a Holy Communion or a Bar Mitzvah. He had a family that loved him. Now he was alone.

How do you end up alone and decomposing like this. This. What *was* this, I wondered, standing staring with my fingers up my nostrils. This is no man. This is garbage. Filthy rotten garbage. Is this what becomes of us. It wasn't just disgusting. It was unbearably disappointing.

I was brought up to think of the human body as a beautiful thing. God's image and likeness. How could God ever look like this.

I'd been reading a lot of T. S. Eliot and had memorized part of *The Waste Land*, "Death by Water." The part about Phlebas the Phoenician, slowly and silently rotting away at the bottom of the sea. Alone and in private, like the man I was looking at now. Experiencing the physical stages of his life in reverse. And I was thinking how, like Phlebas, we're all so much alike. So proud of our appearance and stature, consumed by our petty illusions, then ending up as nothing, coming apart in the *whirlpool*.

That's you, I thought as I stared at the corpse. You're Phlebas. Death certainly has taken you down a few pegs, handsome and tall as you may have been. At that moment I perfectly understood that I was Phlebas, too.

I stood over that corpse for a while; I can't remember how long. I think I was experiencing something Zen Buddhists call brain chatter. A million thoughts all trying to get a word in edgewise. I do know we left the body there for the medical-examiner crew to remove, which they would do only after the detectives had checked everything out. There was no reason to think this was anything but a natural death. It happens every day like this. A natural death, in every sense of the word.

I do remember that my clothes stank all day. And that I skipped lunch in the hospital cafeteria. They were serving gray pot roast. Dead meat. It had a funny smell. Or was that me, smelling myself.

I couldn't sleep the entire week after that call. I was sick at heart, frightened, and in despair. Is that all we're meant to become, I asked myself over and over again. It did me no good later that summer to overhear Felix refer to that call as *the worst one he had ever seen*. It didn't change anything. It didn't help in any way.

When I got back to Vanderbilt that fall to begin my sophomore year, I could hardly study. I couldn't concentrate on anything for more than a few moments. I was a couple of weeks away from my nineteenth birthday. I started drinking more. All times of the day. I went to class half drunk. I slept a lot but not well and ate Burger King four times a day, until my room and my clothing reeked of it and I had to buy a new belt.

I hid all of this as well as I could from Barbara and my family and the few friends I had. Something in me had changed, not for the better, but surely forever.

I had been inside the whirlpool and returned to tell about it.

JESUS SPEAKS

LENNY AND I have been nodding off in the parked ambulance out in the ambulance yard when a call comes in.
Female psycho in Jackson Heights. Not a rush. Got to wake
up and do this thing. The heat is just about intolerable in
here. It's been a slow day. It's much easier to keep moving
when we're fairly busy. We can keep up the momentum
without too much trouble. Always much harder to start
from a dead stop.

Lenny has been on since six this morning, but I have
been here more than thirty hours already, and I am totally
zoned out. How is it that I have been on the job for thirty
hours straight. Isn't there a labor law against this or something. What the hell did I join the union for. Oh yeah, I
forgot. They made me.

It gets worse: I still have six hours to go. Then back tomorrow morning at six for another twelve. Here's how this works.

As far as I know, I'm the only one who pulls thirty-six-hour shifts. This happens because I'm frequently switched from nights to days, and if I'm on a twenty-four-hour Sunday-to-Monday shift, I will go right from that to a twelve-hour day shift, all day Monday. I get this treatment because I'm the relief man, the summer help, so I'm basically expendable in terms of my physical and mental well-being (going fast), my social life (have none), and my morale (have none of that, either). But I suppose it could be worse. Somebody tell me how.

If I'm lucky, on one of these thirty-six-hour shifts, I can sleep in the X-ray room, where it's cool—but I can only do this at night. If I need to catch some z's in the daytime, I have to go into the back of the bus, parked out in the sun, and pull down the shades and lie on the stretcher, drenched in my own sweat. That's where I've been hanging out today. It's miserable and pretty much impossible to sleep, but I've been slipping into mini-comas for a few minutes at a time. Lenny has decided to keep me company out here, and he's reading a catalog in the driver's seat. I think he's been dozing periodically. I've checked out Lenny's reading matter. It's the Miles Kimball of Oshkosh, Wisconsin, catalog. Oh Lenny. You animal.

I sit up on the stretcher and slowly make my way to my seat, and we're off to Jackson Heights. I am right now not even the least bit curious about the nature of this call. All I can think about is getting some sleep. We'll see what it is when we get there.

It's a little old lady. A little old Italian lady. The inside of her apartment looks like how you might picture the gift shop at the Vatican, if it has one. I've never seen so many Blessed Mothers, lenticular Jesuses (who open and shut their eyes as you move your head), and statues of saints and angels. Virtually every square inch of vertical and horizontal space is covered with some type of religious image or sacred objet d'art. She must have spent a fortune on this stuff. (I would say *junk,* but I'm afraid to call it that. You never know.) She speaks English but with a heavy accent. So does my father's mother, but they're not the least bit alike. Nana is pretty swarthy and authentically peasant looking. Also, quite a tough little gnocchi. This woman seems very refined.

She sees me staring at a little statue. *You know who that is,* she says, startling me a bit.

I think I do. He's holding crossed candlesticks, so I take an educated guess: *Saint Blaise.*

She bursts into a wide smile and says, *You such a smart boy. That's right, you right. He was a doctor, just like you.*

I'm not a doctor, Mama. Do you want to go to see one.

No, I'm not going nowhere, she says sweetly but firmly.

Our patient is very pale, with snow-white hair and a somewhat aristocratic mien. Her daughter made the call for an ambulance. *Mom won't take her pills and she's not acting right* —aside from being a religious fanatic—*and I think she needs to see the doctor.* Well, she's not acting *that* funny. We're only a walk or a short cab ride away from Elmhurst General, which is where we'll be taking her. The situation is, as it usually is with so-called psychos, that there is a document that says she can be taken in for observation. I'm sure the party who issued this document has advised the daughter about the proper steps to take—do it right and call for help because you never know how Mom will react. Well, I guess it is good advice. Too many of these calls turn weird.

Dear, it will be okay. We'll just drive you down the street to Elmhurst Hospital and you'll see the doctor and you'll probably be back in no time.

I no ride in no ambulance.

Nothing sweet about her demeanor now. I think she's channeling Nana.

One of the cops chimes in, *Dear, you need to come along with these nice men and you don't want to make a fuss for your neighbors to see, do you.*

They no gonna see me go in no ambulance.

There's the rub. She's embarrassed to ride in an ambulance. So many people are. So many people—even the ones who don't have paper on them that says they have to go—turn RMA (refused medical aid) on us. These are people with all kinds of ailments, most often men with chest pains. We sometimes literally beg them to go, and they still refuse, often with dire consequences. Not the manly thing, you know. But it isn't just the men.

Once Jose and Eddie had a midnight call for a thirteen-year-old girl with abdominal pains. They were sure it was appendicitis. They begged her to go with them. Her parents begged, cried, yelled, and pleaded, and she still wouldn't go. In the early morning a call came in at the same address: possible DOA. This did not have to happen.

But it won't happen in this case. This lady can't RMA, and Lenny and I gently take her by the arms to escort her out into the ambulance, where she is the obvious center of attention of a couple dozen pairs of neighborly eyes. She is silent now, staring straight ahead. She'll never live this down, and I feel sorry for her for that.

She won't sit on the stretcher, so I sit her down on the bench next to me. Her daughter says she'll meet us there. I guess she doesn't want to be seen riding in an ambulance, either.

Mom is suddenly very quiet, with her eyes closed. We're under way to EGH. Her eyes are opening very slowly, and only the whites are visible. I have to stifle a smirk. We see the old white eye a lot, and it always means one thing: phony baloney. We see it the most when people are trying to fake unconsciousness. Very often in family disputes, where someone collapses in a fake faint or when someone is pretending they've been knocked out by a blow or other injury. You open their eyelids to take a look at their pupils and whoa, what's this—there are no pupils. They've rolled up their eyeballs in a creditable imitation of a voodoo celebrant in maximum mojo mode.

The thing is, when you're really out, or dead, your eyes

relax into the pupils-straight-ahead position. So if you're planning to fake being out or dead anytime soon, keep this in mind and try to stare straight ahead.

Her eyes are all white and scary when I begin to ask her the personal information we need to fill out our pink call sheets. What's your full name, date of birth, all the standard stuff. I'm in the middle of a sentence when we have the following *conversation*. She speaks in a firm, loud, and surprisingly unaccented monotone:

I AM THE VOICE OF JESUS CHRIST.

LET GO A THIS WOMAN RIGHT NOW.

SHE AIN'T GOT NOTHING WRONG WITH HER.

LET GO A THIS WOMAN RIGHT NOW.

Dear, when is your birthday…

I AM THE VOICE OF JESUS CHRIST…

DO *NOT* INTERRUPT.

I've only cried a couple of times on the ambulance, but those were tears of pathos rather than suppressed mirth, which is now the case. Lenny is hearing all this and looking back. There seems to be the faint outline of an actual expression on his normally blank face. I would have to describe it as a smile. Lenny has *smiled*. The voice of Jesus has worked another miracle. The Miracle of Roosevelt Avenue.

Ma'am, you need to tell me how old you are. We're approaching the Roosevelt Avenue–Seventy-Fourth Street IRT elevated station. We'll be passing under it. For a split second, I see her pupils flip back down. She sees where we are.

I AM THE VOICE OF JESUS CHRIST.

IF YOU DO NOT LET THIS WOMAN OUT I GONNA MAKE THESE TRACKS FALL DOWN AND KILL ALL A YOU.

Lenny taps the brakes almost imperceptibly when he hears what she—I mean Jesus—has to say. Not enough to come to a stop but enough to slow us down so he can digest the full import of what our onboard prophet has just said. When Lenny touches the brakes, I burst out roaring with laughter. Completely out of control. I was trying so hard to keep it in. Now I'm whimpering into my elbow with high-pitched laughter, wiping off the tears on the short sleeve of my shirt. Through all this, I have to say that I am actually just a *little* curious as to what will happen when we go under the El tracks, as we must, to get to EGH.

It is impossible not to look up as we approach the overhead rails.

Our patient is smiling smugly, eyes shut tight. She's waiting for the doom she knows will claim us all. As we ease our way under the elevated tracks, a passing number 7 train, as if on cue, produces a racket loud enough to give us a start. But we emerge safe and sound. Her smug smile turns into an impassive mask. Neither she nor Jesus has another word to say to us.

I can't believe Lenny was spooked enough by the voice of Jesus to hit the brakes. He's not a Catholic. He's not even a Christian. But I guess it really doesn't matter.

When it's Jesus talking, you pay attention.

THE LEAST WE CAN DO

THIS IS MORE like it. It's unusually quiet tonight, thank God. It's past midnight, and we've only had a couple of calls since we got on at 6:00 p.m. Looks like I may get some sleep in the meat-locker-cold X-ray room. I can't wait. I am so exhausted all the time because of this job. The hours are really killing me. The worst part about getting *some* sleep is you're always on edge. It's rare that you can sleep more than fifteen or thirty minutes without a call coming in. On rare occasions, you can get a couple of hours or more. But it only helps a little. This interrupted sleep cycle has really messed me up, to the point where I can't sleep well even when I'm home, after working twelve hours all night or for twenty-four—sometimes thirty-six—hours straight.

I'm on tonight with Andy. We get along great. We're both aware that this might be a night to catch a few winks, and it has us in a jolly frame of mind. Like they say, *It's the simple things.* But there's a problem. We're both so stoked at the prospect of sleep that we're not sleepy. So we're sitting up talking when a call comes in. It's a man down—on a ship.

A *ship*. Man down. Don't they say *man overboard* when it's a ship. *Why not call the Coast Guard,* Andy says, only half kidding. Do we even *do* ships. I certainly never have. It's almost 2:00 a.m., and the call is at one of the piers in the East River, so we'd better get moving. It's about as long a run as we ever make, and it will take a bit of time to get there, even with negligible 2:00 a.m. traffic.

I've never been down here before, and Andy says he hasn't, either. There are no police to be seen, which is unusual. Maybe they have more pressing business elsewhere or maybe the call just got lost in the shuffle. We can't wait for them. We've parked the bus behind a building that seems to house equipment and the office section of the piers. There's a lone man waiting here, apparently for us, because he's walking over even before Andy shuts off the engine. He says he'll take us to the ship, with a slight accent that I can't immediately place. He says a crewman has hurt his back and needs to be looked at in a hospital. How did he hurt his back. The man isn't sure.

We turn the corner of the building, and there's the ship. Holy Mother of God. It is absolutely huge. Stories and stories high, towering against the Manhattan skyline. It's just gigantic. The Mount Everest of all ships. Am I challenged to make an ascent. Hell no. Why not. To deliberately misinterpret George Mallory: *Because it's there.*

I'm afraid of heights. Not heights per se, but *being* in high places. They make me sweaty, panicky, and disoriented. The usual. I've been afraid of heights all my life and take little comfort in the fact that I share this fear with millions.

The closer we walk to this natant Godzilla, the bigger it gets and the sicker I feel. We're at the edge of the pier, and the black water is far, far below. *Way* down there. So we're already pretty high up—and the ship climbs monumentally higher from there. She's riding high—the red paint that marks her waterline is well out of the water. She's empty of cargo.

Our guide sees me staring at the ship and must be reading my mind, because he starts to tell me about it. It's a cement ship from Sweden. What's that now. At this hour of the morning, or probably at any time of the day, the idea of importing cement from Sweden just doesn't make sense. Anyway, this explains his accent. He nods and points to a very high spot on the ship as a signal that we need to get on up there. *Is that where he is.* The man nods.

It gets worse. Our guide (he says his name is Jim, which doesn't sound very Swedish) is leading us to the gangplank. Oh holy shit. It's really long and really narrow and really flimsy, and it slopes up to the ship from the side of the dock. There are thin ropes on either side. It's barely wide enough for a normal-sized person to walk on—and Andy and I are far from what you would call normal sized. Each of us weighs in excess of two hundred pounds, with Andy well in excess of that. Not fat, stocky. Heavyset. Okay, maybe a little fat. So we're heavy and wide is the point. That water is way down there. We have to go across. There is no other way onto the ship.

Not only is this one of my worst nightmares, sprung to synapse-triggering, adrenaline-spurting life, but I realize I will have to repeat it, maybe three more times, depending on what equipment we will have to bring up from the ambulance to remove the injured sailor. Imagine the most flexible diving board you've ever been on. Then imagine it with four-hundred-plus pounds of human flesh flexing it up and down. Then imagine it being, I don't know, maybe forty feet or more from the water's surface. You may be close to forming an image of our journey across the gangplank.

This is absolutely and without a doubt shaping up as one of the most terrifying experiences of my nineteen-year life. I can't even imagine what may be yet to come. Maybe I won't have to worry about that. Maybe it will end right here, tonight.

Our patient is way the hell up in a room somewhere at the very top of the bridge, which is like a small skyscraper at the rear of the ship. Like a city stuck on top of a boat. On a ship like this, as on most ships, there are no staircases, just ship ladders, nearly vertical steps with handrails on either side. The kind the navy guys slide down in the movies when the captain sounds general quarters. What fun they seem to have doing that.

Andy and I look at each other. How are we going to bring this guy down these ladders, much less climb them with our stuff: stretcher or backboard. It has to be one or the other, since we'd never transport a back injury any other way than flat. Well, let's get up there and see what we've got.

Up and up and up and many ladders later, here we are— and someone is not a happy Swedish camper.

Our patient is on his side, slightly bent, lying on the floor. His name is Sten. He won't let anybody move him. He won't let anybody even touch him. Jim says nobody has, although this is clearly not where he got hurt and he has to have been moved, which could have caused worse damage. I think this must be Jim's office area or something. No one knows what happened—they just found him like this. So we don't know if it's a possible fracture or he just bent over and slipped a disc. Sten isn't talking, either. Just yowling at the top of his lungs.

Sten is experiencing what, in my brief and purely empirical study of the subject, I have come to term *maximum pain*. Maximum pain is scream inducing and will not abate without the advent of shock or drugs or death. This is pain during which the patient is fully conscious and probably aware of the fact that this pain is not *normal* pain and will not necessarily go away without dramatic intervention. So there is terror in the screams. Because of these criteria, even though it is intense and scream inducing, I don't include labor during childbirth in this category. I understand the pain of childbirth is horrendous, but it has peaks and valleys and, of course, hopefully, a wonderful reward when it's over.

The kind of pain I'm seeing has no peaks or valleys or reward at the end. It's all peaks. My list so far of things that cause maximum pain: burns, kidney stones, and a good many back and neck injuries. Other than treating screamers as gently as we can and trying to keep our own nervous systems in check, there is absolutely nothing we can do. We have nothing to give them. No drugs. None of those little morphine syrettes you see the medics give the wounded in war movies. Not even aspirin. Not one thing.

We need to get Sten to the hospital as soon as we can. Do we climb back down all the stairs and over the (insert expletive here) gangplank and back with our stuff. What *stuff* do we bring with us. The stretcher. The backboard. If we bring the backboard, we'll have to literally lash him to the board—we have straps for that in the ambulance, like seat belts.

Andy and I agree—there is no time to lose, and it's questionable whether we can make it up the ladders with either the stretcher or the backboard.

Jim, do you guys have a hoist or something.

No.

Do you have a stretcher on board.

No. All we have is this. It's a folding aluminum wheelchair, the kind with the tiny rubber wheels and red vinyl padding, virtually identical to the one we have on the ambulance.

Does Jim have any straps. Yes, he has those, too.

Andy is deep in thought, looking at the chair, then at me, then at Sten. And he makes a decision that makes me glad I'm not him. *We can take Sten down strapped into this chair.*

This is definitely not protocol and extremely risky. Sten is screaming a little less now—I check his pulse, and it's still strong, and his color is good. In fact, it's great—his face is red as a tomato from yelling. *Jim, please ask Sten if he can move his feet.* We ask Jim to ask Sten, because we assume Sten has no English—but he understands us, and it seems to help him focus a little, between his spasms of agony. Sten obligingly moves his feet. At least he isn't already paralyzed. If we make him paralyzed by bending him to fit into the chair, God help us both and Sten, too. Andy seems to think it's an acceptable risk. Best not to ask Sten what he thinks, just now.

We're going to have to move you, Sten. We're going to put you on this chair and carry you down. We need you to cooperate. Can you do that. It's going to hurt. We hope it will hurt. If it stops hurting, we're all in big trouble. Sten gets a very thoughtful look on his face and grimly nods okay. I'm thinking that he's thinking, How are these two bozos going to do this. So at least we're all on the same page with that. *None* of us has a clue. We're just going to have to do it.

Sten screams when we lift him. Horror-movie caliber. Bloodcurdling. My nervous system is getting the workout of a lifetime tonight. Now he's in a sitting position in the chair, groaning loudly. We cover him with a blanket and strap his arms to the sides of the chair as well as we can—there are no armrests. We strap his legs. Bitter experience teaches us that, in the patient-toting business, loose arms can spell disaster when a panicked patient reaches out for a handrail, banister, or newel post, and everyone goes down the stairs in an avalanche of arms, legs, brainpans, and spinal columns.

Andy and I don't have to ask each other how we're going to do this, at this point. I will take the bottom and go down backward, and he will take the top, as always. Sometimes, when there are cops on the scene, I'll get a helpful hand in the form of a fist wrapped around my belt, pushing in and upward against the small of my back. Not this time.

Also, this time, I will be able to use only one arm on the chair. The other will have to hold the railing. Andy will go down face forward, holding the top of the chair with one hand and the railing with the other. It all sounds pretty cut-and-dried in theory. In reality, it will take everything we've got to pull it off.

No one I work with at St. John's is what you'd call Charles Atlas material or even close. We're as strong as we have to be. Some of the people we have to carry—when it's possible for only two to make the carry—are *very* heavy. A lot of them live in walk-up buildings, several stories up. We have our techniques, but at the end of the day, it comes down to strength, balance, and that secret ingredient, adrenaline. I have to think that this indispensable hormone may be good for at least a 50 percent increase in carrying power.

And I am going to need all the carrying power I can muster to get Sten down these ladders backward, one-handed, then over the bouncing gangplank (now to be burdened with around six hundred pounds) and into our waiting ambulance. I should have plenty of adrenaline available, because I'm scared shitless.

We begin our descent. Thankfully, Sten has settled down. Abject terror can temporarily override even the worst pain, and I have to think Sten is even more terrified at the thought of making this trip—from this height, facing forward into the night air, with arms and legs immobilized—than we are. So is this your first trip to the Big Apple, Mr. Sten. How do you like the view.

I'm trying not to think about the height or the fact that there's no one behind me or what will happen if Andy loses his grip or balance or if Sten frees an arm and grabs the railing. I'm trying not to think at all as I feel my way backward down each step. It's exhausting, and we have to rest after each ladder. We're finally down. Oh Jesus: we're going to walk the plank. At least if this is our time to go, it will be with some sense of the romance of the high seas.

Well, we made it. Thank God—I sincerely mean that, God.

Move your feet for us, Sten. He still can. One more tricky part to go. *The Unfolding of Sten.* Could be a good title for an Ingmar Bergman movie. If we can get him laid out more or less flat on the stretcher without any obvious bad effects—like paralysis, for instance—we're almost home free. We begin unfolding. Sten resumes screaming. Oh man. At last, Sten is out flat, if not cold. His screaming has stopped. We take our time strapping him down and lift him very deliberately into the back of the ambulance. One more time:

Sten, can you move your feet.

Yes.

Ready to go.

On the way, Sten asks for a cigarette. This is taboo in the ambulance, because of the oxygen. Just something you don't even think about doing—and we all smoke like fiends.

Sorry, Sten, you can't smoke in the ambulance because of the oxygen. Sten says nothing. Then he says just one word.

Please.

It's hot out, even at this hour, and all the windows are open. There is no air conditioning on this bus. Andy is driving slowly. I've never seen him drive so slowly. I'd say we're going no more than fifteen miles per hour. Even creeping along at this speed, we feel the bumps clearly. Every street in the city is made of bumps, having been paved, dug up, and repaved more times than anyone can count. The suspension on this vehicle is just a degree or two more advanced than that of a Radio Flyer wagon. One bump = one outcry. Sten is going through hell. We've got nothing for him. The least we can do is let him smoke.

Once again, I'm thankful I'm not the senior man. I don't have to decide whether we're going to break another unbreakable rule tonight.

Andy slows down even further, almost to a stop, and turns to speak to me. I guess he heard Sten say the magic word.

Give him a butt, Mike. And give me one, while you're at it.

SILENCE IS GOLDEN

IT IS SO dark out this morning. It should be lighter—the solstice was only a couple of weeks ago. I'm just about dead right now; we've been going crazy with calls all night, and none of us, on either ambulance, has gotten any sleep at all. The Zombies of Queens Boulevard. That's us. It's a little after four. Not too much longer now. Even though our shift nominally ends at 6:00 a.m., we all try to relieve one another no later than 5:30. It's silly, but it does create some kind of artificial carrot to keep us going a little longer. It's just a game, but we are simple working folk, and we live by games like this.

Call. Possible DOA in Forest Hills. I'm on with Enrico. I can't say I've ever heard him say more than a few syllables at a time, and that only when sorely pressed. He's short and dark and I think he's from Naples. For all I know he has an accent, but I haven't heard enough actual speech come out of him to tell. He looks like the love child of Perry Como and some mythic entity, maybe a gnome. He has that gnarly

89

gnome face and Perry's perfectly sculpted, razor-cut hair. In a certain light, this combination of incongruous elements can be strangely fascinating.

Enrico smokes guinea stinkers all day long. Either smokes them or has one stuck like a permanent fixture in the corner of his mouth, like Big Al. These things do look kind of cool, but they're nasty, made from the worst possible tobacco you could imagine. One morning things were slow and we were all outside in the yard talking trash when Enrico asked me if I wanted to try one. He didn't actually ask in words. He merely held the open pack toward me with one cigar extended for me to take. He stared at me, waiting for me to respond. Sure, why not.

I had been smoking for a while, mostly pipes at school (but tons of cigarettes since working on the ambulance). Some of the tobacco is pretty strong, particularly a brand in a can that comes from Scotland, called Four Square Curlies. Several times I got too dizzy smoking this mixture to study—reason 15 in my *I'll Study Later* catalog. The dizziness would pass after an hour or so, and I would then move on to an alternative reason not to study.

A lot of first-time smokers get horribly sick from their initial exposure to nicotine—which is not surprising, given that it's one of the deadlier poisons out there. I prided myself on the fact that I never had. So when Enrico offered me a Palumbo to smoke there in the ambulance yard, I lit up without a second's hesitation. All three of my coworkers watched me intently. I made the international sign for *no big deal*—the downturned mouth, with raised eyebrows and shrugged shoulders. Enrico spoke, which startled us all a little: *Wyn-chounhale*. Huh. Oh. *Why don't I inhale.* Okay, fine, if it will make you happy. I took three or four deep drags. That was all it took. Everyone looked at me with grins of evil anticipation. It didn't take long for them to get what they were waiting for.

I spent most of the day, when I could, lying on the stretcher in the back of 434. It was a horrible kind of sick. Nauseated and dizzy; mostly dizzy. It wasn't like a hangover. I didn't feel that throwing up would do any good. I actually wanted to throw up, but it wouldn't come. I wondered if anybody who smoked these things ever did inhale them or just sucked on them, unlit, as some sort of big-boy Binky. This episode closed the book on my Palumbo Period.

Today I'm virtually comatose from lack of sleep. We're on the way, Enrico and I, to the DOA in Forest Hills. I like going to Forest Hills. It's a nice neighborhood for the most part, and you don't see the kind of depressing living conditions you see in other areas. There's the projects, which you'd expect to be rough, given the poverty. What you don't expect is the squalor you sometimes find in supposedly solid blue-collar neighborhoods. I can take a lot. Blood, gore, the entire catalog of horrifying things that can happen to a human body. What often bothers me more than seeing how people die is seeing how they live.

Caruso stops the bus without a word. In we go.

It is very dark in the apartment. One light is on, in the kitchen. Outside, morning twilight is just getting started. The best way to describe the light outside and inside is *murky*. There seem to be an awful lot of people here for this hour of the morning. There's a woman about forty. There are two uniforms. And there are two guys in suits. I simply cannot integrate all of this information, and I'm too tired to ask. Let them just tell me what's going on, for once. Lead on. One of the cops points me toward a door, which turns out to be a bedroom. I can tell he's not coming with, and neither is Enrico. Okay, let's get this over with. Inside, there are two more men in suits. Are they from a funeral home or something.

There's a dead man in the bed. Very clearly dead. He's backlit by the murky light coming in through a window. Indigo-blue light. I can barely see. Why doesn't somebody turn on a light for Pete's sake. The woman has come in, and she's standing by my shoulder. I guess she's waiting for me to say something or ask some questions, questions someone like me would ask in a situation like this.

I'm about to launch into our usual *patter*. This patter consists of small talk we make to keep the next of kin from going primal on us. It's designed to distract them momentarily, like when you shine a bright light in the eyes of a frog that you want to gig, if you're into that. Needless to say, Caruso doesn't do patter.

The patter usually goes something like this: Bless his heart, was he suffering from any condition, did he have it long, was he being seen by a doctor, et cetera. Very clinical and pretty much irrelevant. Yet it usually lulls loved ones long enough for us to get the information we need and get out of there before the shit hits the fan.

I've been staring at this body and seeing nothing but a corpse as the woman stands patiently and silently beside me. She is almost surely the spouse, but I never assume any-thing. Before I turn to patter her up, as my eyes are becom-ing adjusted to the dark—or maybe it's getting lighter out-side, probably both—I see something I hadn't seen when I first came in. I come wide awake. Fast. There is dark mate-rial on the pillow under and around the back of the man's head. Ah. Blood and brains.

I shift my eyes down the bed, without moving my head. I don't want it to seem too obvious that I'm scrutinizing the scene carefully for the first time. Peeking out from under the blanket and sheet, barely visible, is the tip of a rifle barrel.

On the window-lit side of the man's head, just under his jaw, there's a perfectly round, dark red hole. Mystery solved. The suits are detectives, of course. Our DOA either shot himself—or not—which is why they're here. At any rate, he was shot and he's dead and we're done. What an ass I almost made of myself. I came *that* close to pattering up his wife as to what she thought the cause of death was.

I've decided as of this call that Caruso may be onto something.

THOSE GUYS

WHO DOESN'T LOVE a good gangster story. Those hard-bitten, good/bad-but-not-evil guys we all love to hate. Slaughtering one another wholesale. Standing up to the law: giving a big fat middle finger to the cops, the courts, the finks, the wardens, and the screws. You dirty rats. Come and get me, coppers.

Bad guys are a fact of life in Queens. We all know a few people we are reasonably sure are connected. I grew up with friends whose dads are probably in. I don't ask, and they don't have to lie about it. They live their lives and so do I and we all get along fine.

Some people think those guys only hurt their own. But anyone who has ever run a bar or restaurant or done commercial construction knows better. Sure, it's rare for an ordinary civilian to get seriously hurt or killed as long as they do as they're expected. But if you're in business with the bad guys, whether it's drugs or loan-sharking or prostitution or even running a pizza place or uniform service, you know what your life is worth if you do something to piss them off.

When they do get pissed off, they leave their calling cards at random all over town. My father had a car parked for several days near the gas station, nearly blocking the driveway. It reeked. The cops finally came, and there was a decomposing body in the trunk. I guess they didn't have time to run the car over to La Guardia or Kennedy.

Big Al and I once had a call in a vacant lot. A man bound hand and foot and beaten to death while sitting in a chair. Might have been shot, as well, but he was too messed up for us to see any bullet holes. And the holes those guys leave are really small; they do love their .22s. Quiet, unobtrusive, and oh so effective, especially up close. No sloppy exit wounds, either.

As I say, it's rare that they hurt a civilian for no apparent reason. Rare, but not unheard of. The guy I'm looking at now is proof of that. We may even find out what happened, if he can stop sobbing and babbling incoherently long enough to get his story out.

We're up on a hill overlooking Manhattan, on a road roughly parallel to the Long Island Expressway, looking west, just before the Midtown Tunnel. You've probably seen it many times in still photos and movies. On the right, there's a big redbrick church. We're surrounded by Calvary Cemetery, which covers well over three hundred acres. At least a few of my relatives are buried here. Along with millions of others.

We got this call as a man down.

I would say he's about as down as a man can get before being all the way down. Like down-in-the-ground down.

He is a bloody mess. Looks like he has several fractured bones, including a few fingers, one radius-ulna combo, a wrist, maybe his jaw, and very likely a good-sized fracture or two in his skull. His nose is crushed, and the orbit of one eye appears to be seriously deformed, even though right now it's hard to tell how seriously, because of the swelling. Looks like some of his teeth have been knocked out. His mouth is full of blood, so it's hard to tell if the missing teeth are old missing teeth or newly missing. He has pissed himself copiously, although some of the dark staining in his crotch could be blood. He is as terrified as anyone we've ever picked up. I'm trying to think if I've ever seen anyone beaten this badly who was still alive. I don't think I have.

I do know that I've seen people beaten not *nearly* this badly who were dead.

One thing is clear just by looking at him. Whoever did this knew what they were doing. He was beaten very carefully, with maximum attention to efficiency and detail. With just enough force to maim him as much as possible and yet not enough to kill. There were well-honed skills involved here. It's actually kind of impressive, in a sick way.

I'm wondering if he'll be able to settle down enough to tell us the story, but I don't think so. We can't wait—he needs to get treatment, stat. Doesn't matter. The cops know what happened because someone came forward and told them: someone naïve enough not to know enough to keep his mouth shut.

He'll probably realize what he did just before he goes to sleep tonight and break out in a cold sweat. I mean just before he *tries* to go to sleep.

Apparently there was a big funeral procession heading to a burial at Calvary. Because it was so big, the cars carrying the attendees were really spread out. As is sometimes the case even with ordinary funerals, red lights are more or less ignored. The cops say our victim was driving west in a path that took him directly across the southerly direction of the procession. He had a green light. The spacing between the cars in the cortege had gotten so wide that our victim must not have even been aware he was cutting off a funeral.

But this was *not* an ordinary funeral.

As soon as our patient had crossed the street, a black sedan pulled out of the procession and followed him, proceeding to overtake him and pull in front of his car, forcing him to screech to a halt. Then out popped four men, up popped the trunk, and out popped the baseball bats and ax handles. The rest, as they say, is history.

So much for the bad guys not picking on innocents.

The bad guys do what they want to do, when they want to do it.

That's what makes them the bad guys.

A HOUSE LIKE MINE

WHEN I WAS in the Boy Scouts studying knots, we used to make hangman's nooses. We were told they had to have exactly thirteen turns. I always thought that was so melodramatic. Or, at least, redundant. As if you had to include a symbol for bad luck just to underline the fact that this knot was going to be used to kill someone.

I could never get my hangman's noose to work right. I mean theoretically, of course. The ropes we used for knot practice were too soft, like clothesline, and I believe you need stiff rope for a good hangman's noose, so the free end will slide easily through the loops. A brand-new sisal rope, the kind that's all bristly with fibers, would be best. I wonder if the *pros* reuse them. If so, they would have to be adjustable. Maybe they have laws against reuse. They used to hang people in New York but switched to the electric chair and last used that in 1963. There are still professional hangmen in the United States and elsewhere, though. And I thought *my* job was bad.

They say it's quick—it's supposed to break your neck. That's what the hangman's noose is for. It's constructed to abruptly snap the head to the side, to sever the spinal column. But that's an *official* hanging, an execution, with a gallows and a trapdoor and the whole nine yards.

But there are a lot more *unofficial* hangings, where a hangman's noose isn't employed—suicides, homicides, lynchings. Hangings where it's doubtful the deceased had the dubious luxury of getting a nice clean broken neck instead of being slowly strangled by his or her own weight.

I'm on with Fred, and we've got a possible DOA in Woodside. Man hung. We don't usually get that much information, so we have a general idea what to expect this time. Actually, I'm sure Fred has a general idea, or even a very specific idea, since he's been to hangings before, and I haven't.

The only mental images I can come up with are from the photographs of hanged persons I've seen in books. And from descriptions in literature and the bull people shoot when they don't know what they're talking about. For one: they say the eyes and tongue bulge out. I haven't seen that in the photographs. I guess it's possible.

If it works right, there should be no bulging eyes or extended tongue. It should be no different than any ordinary, everyday, lethal broken neck. And that I *have* seen. It's intended to be quick, but I don't think it's instantaneous. Very few deaths are. And of course there are the *Ripley's Believe It or Not!*-type cases, when it hasn't worked and the intended victim has gone free, or so the stories go. Interestingly, I've never read one about someone who lived and ended up quadriplegic. I guess there's nothing Ripley-esque about that—doesn't make for a very good story.

There are two police cars here, and one of them is unmarked, so my first guess is they think this hanging may be—make that *is*—suspicious. *He's down in the cellar, you guys,* says the officer who's been waiting for us. *Follow me.* We do.

This is a pretty nice house, not much different from our house in Bayside. In fact, it's almost identical—one of the houses Sears used to sell out of a catalog. Apparently it had all kinds of models, from modest ones like this to Tara look-alikes.

This one is from the midteens. The Hillrose style. For about fifteen hundred dollars, you got the whole *kit* delivered to your site. Assuming the site was prepared, all you needed to do was put it together or find someone who could. Like a big scale model but with stuff like plumbing and wiring on the inside and no decals to mess up. How well it went depended on the *model builder's* skill in putting everything together. This Sears house is a good one. Better built than ours, I think.

How do I know all this. My parents' neighbors found an old Sears house catalog and gave it to them one Christmas. That's how.

The fact that this place is laid out like my own house is giving me a slight case of the creeps. We're going down into the basement, and it's as if my mother has sent me down to get some potatoes or something. Except that none of my family members are here. In fact, other than us and the cops, there is no one at home apart from the gentleman in the basement, hanging quietly from one of the joists, wearing blue boxers, a white T-shirt, and no shoes.

If I had a buck for every dead man we've found wearing almost exactly the same outfit, I'd be able to treat the entire ER to pizza. Blue boxers and a white T-shirt. Or white sleeveless undershirt. It has to be a really unlucky wardrobe option. Or maybe it's not an option. Maybe it's more of an omen. Like a dead man's hand in poker.

There are a couple of bare light bulbs hanging in the basement and lots of shelves, tools, and cubbies, all exceptionally neat and orderly.

In fact, *neat and orderly* is how I would have to describe this entire scene. That is one major way in which this house differs from my own. Not that we're slobs. But there are six of us. I don't think anyone else lives here except for this man. *Lived* here.

The deceased is a forty-four-year-old Hispanic male, according to the ID the detectives have found upstairs in the wallet in his pants. Neatly folded, I bet.

He's a slightly built man. It's hard to tell from where I stand, but I'd guess he's no more than five foot one, and I doubt he weighs much more than a hundred pounds. He looks like he could have been a jockey. A very nice-looking human being, as most jockeys seem to be. Clean-cut; symmetrical features. Almost pretty. Not an ounce of fat. What a waste of a fine body.

Since this is my first hanging, I have no standard of comparison against which to judge what I'm looking at, but I have to think it's a little out of the ordinary. For one thing, our victim has used white electrical wire instead of rope. He has somehow managed to hang a loop of wire from a joist, creating a U shape with just enough room to squeeze in his head. It looks like he had thought this out; maybe even measured it off. This man's whole environment—probably his entire life—seems to have been thought out and measured off. There was just enough space for him to squeeze his head into the loop and not enough for it to easily come back out—the rear of his head being blocked by the joist, once his head was through.

It looks like he must have stood on the stool that's lying all the way across the room. If I had to guess, I'd say this is why the patrolmen called in the detectives. That stool is pretty far from the victim. Was it actually kicked by the hanged man or planted there by someone else. Common sense tells me no killer would have planted it way across the room. But maybe this was a very subtle killer who *wanted* us to think that. Hard to keep my mind from wandering.

It strikes me again how orderly the whole scene is. This man is hanging there so neatly, absolutely plumb, precisely symmetrical. The wire has cut deeply into his throat below his jaw, outlining his jaw perfectly. It must have crushed his trachea almost immediately. Even so, he would have had an agonizing death as he choked. But he looks very peaceful. His eyes and mouth are closed. No bulges in evidence. No visible signs of stress. He could almost be asleep, except that he has hanged himself to death in his basement in his underwear.

On the floor below where his feet hang suspended, merely eighteen inches or so above the painted concrete, there is a perfectly pristine puddle of urine. Even it looks neat and orderly. No muss, no fuss. Except for that one spot, the floor looks clean enough to eat off of. I wonder if he kicked his legs. Could be, but that would have had no effect on the perfection of the puddle. The urine would have been released gently, perimortem.

There seems to be some question as to whether or not we should take him down, now that the detectives are finished having their look. They're calling this a suicide, as I thought they would. So what do we do now.

I have to turn to Fred on this one. *Cut him down,* he says. It sounds so dramatic, like we're acting in some Saturday-morning western and he's a rustler, lynched by an out-of-control posse.

All the while we've been here, I've been scanning the basement for a pair of wire cutters, just in case. Not only do I find a pair, there are *six pairs,* mounted on pegboard, in size order.

With painted outlines no less, so there would be no mistake about where to put them back.

I'M A DADDY

I'M LYING IN 433 trying to sleep, but it's very hot in here even at one in the morning. How do I feel about things in general. Not so good but not that bad, either. This job affects people in what seems to be a set number of predictable ways, none of them particularly good. Some of them get hardened (which is not good for them *or* the patients). Some of them go numb. Some get angry at what the world—what life—does to us all. Some get depressed. Some freak out. Some end up with a combination of all of these effects.

Right now, put me in the *numb* column.

Some of them, the freak-outs, just can't take it. I'm thinking about a guy named Jerry, in particular. He worked with us a few weeks. Maybe a month. He was a very religious Catholic.

I had heard that Jerry had a thing where he'd hold patients' hands and pray with them while they were in the moving ambulance and even on into the ER. Didn't matter if they were Catholic. Or even Christian. Or even able to understand what was going on. There were complaints. Praying with people who are afraid they're going to die can terrify them if they're not expecting it. And besides, there are priests at the hospital who can do that with them when we get there.

Don't get me wrong. There's a place for reverence. I'll never forget the time we had a woman down, struck by a car, lying on her back on a sidewalk on Astoria Boulevard. As we walked up, I heard a voice I hadn't heard since I was about seven years old. There was a priest crouched over the woman, giving her the final sacrament. I heard this voice, deep and resonant, almost hypnotic. I knew immediately it was one of the priests who had been at Sacred Heart in Bayside when I was a kid, who had long ago moved on, as the best ones usually do. *Father Sherman,* I asked. It was. He was focused on the woman down and didn't look up. That voice. That beautiful, deep, soft, comforting voice. If I were on my way out, that's what I'd want to hear.

But there are some kinds of prayers nobody wants to hear. Maybe even God. These are the kind Jerry would blurt out when he brought in a bad one. Loud and fast, in the middle of the emergency room, in front of all the staff and the waiting patients. Some of them are here for *sprained thumbs,* Jerry. Leave them out of this. It's bad enough you just trundled a gore-encrusted incipient corpse past them at eye level. Give us all a break, man.

We got our break, and I was there to see it.

Jerry and Lenny came in with an overdose. The man was

blue. He was technically dead, but these cases can surprise you. Sometimes with a shot of adrenaline they spring back to life. It's impressive and, in its own way, a miracle. But it's one of those so-called miracles of modern medicine. Not the spiritual kind that has no explanation.

I guess Jerry didn't know yet about these miraculous re-animations. As far as he was concerned, this was a DOA. The minute he delivered his patient to the ER, he dropped to his knees in front of everyone and started praying at the top of his lungs. Shortly after he started, a large and imposing figure loomed in the corridor at the other end of the ER. A nun. This immediately caught Jerry's attention, and he stopped spluttering and looked up at her. She gave him the dreaded sign that anyone who has ever gone to parochial school knows all too well: the beckoning index finger, *come with me, young man* sign. Jerry got up. All eyes were on him as he and Sister Mary Doom walked down the corridor and out of sight. In the case of Jerry, out of sight permanently.

Or so I thought, because that was the last time I saw him myself.

It turned out they kept Jerry and placed him on some kind of probation. I heard the terms were that he couldn't touch (hold hands) or pray with the patients in transit (or otherwise) and he had to remove himself from the ER immediately after dropping off a patient. Any praying was to be done out of earshot of anybody except God. He had to work with Pete, the boss, while he was being evaluated. I think things worked out for a week or so. Then something happened to poor pious Jerry that I have always prayed (figuratively—*silently*) would never happen to me.

Pete and Jerry were on a call. It was a middle-aged male DOA in a home in Forest Hills. The family went hysterical when Pete turned and told them the man was gone. Pete was consoling them with the usual patter when Jerry apparently decided to check things out for himself. He felt a pulse. *I got a pulse,* he shouted, right out loud. No filter whatsoever. The family's hysteria turned to outright mania. All directed at Pete. *How could you be so stupid. Get him to the hospital. You dumb son of a bitch.* The word *lawsuit* was heard—multiple times.

All this happened because Jerry had pressed too hard on the dead man's wrist and felt his own pulse.

This is so easy to do—and it's one of the things I fear above all others—proclaiming someone dead when they're not. Or vice versa. Maybe you wouldn't think so, but it's hard to determine if someone is dead on the spot, on the scene, with everyone standing around in their agony. All eyes are on you. You have to be sure. You also have to be *right*.

Pete and Jerry were forced to transport the corpse to St. John's with the family posse trailing behind. The second they got in the door, Pete turned to Jerry and fired him on the spot. Frankly, I'm surprised Pete didn't beat Jerry senseless. I have no doubt that was on his mind.

No one has seen or heard from Jerry since.

So, with Jerry's story as a memorable object lesson: I'd rather be numb than freak out. Right now, only food makes me happy—until I step on a scale. We eat so much on this job you'd think I'd be a lot happier. Somebody tell a joke.

Here comes Jose with a call. It's a maternity, in Woodside. My first. A *rush* maternity. Is there any other kind.

Are you awake.

I am now, Jose.

We're off. On the way, between wholly unnecessary bursts of the siren, Jose leans over to tell me something. *You gonna be a daddy, baby.*

I'm going to be a daddy. I've been waiting for this.

Everyone I ride with busts my chops about the fact that I've never been on a maternity call. They're constantly pulling the old *Which hand do you cut the cord with, kid,* on me.

I fell for it once. *The right hand.*

Oh really, they'd say. *We always use scissors.*

Ha-ha. Not funny the first time or any of the two- or three-dozen times after that.

I've been told by everyone that maternities are pretty simple unless something happens that *isn't* simple, like a breech. You stand by and wait for the baby to come out while spouting encouraging phrases to the mother and whoever else is there. When the baby comes, you cradle it with both hands and lay it on the bed or stretcher or floor—wherever Mom has decided to get the job done. Of course, wherever it is, you put clean linens down first. This is New York City, not a beet field in Omsk. Then you lay it gently on Mom.

You're supposed to wait a bit for the umbilical cord to achieve detumescence. I love that word, but I almost never get to use it in a sentence, and I've yet to see it in a crossword. It means *get limp*. At first, the cord is full of blood and so stiff I'm told it could snap like a fresh green bean, although I'm pretty sure no one has tried this. After a bit, when it's limp, you're supposed to *milk* the blood down toward the baby and measure off a length about the width of your hand with fingers held loosely apart and then clamp it down above your hand and cut it off at least an inch above the clamp.

The clamps are nasty little things. They look like they're made out of nylon or some other kind of plastic. They're springy and have teeth and a little lock at the end, so when they're on, they stay put. After clamping, you give junior or sis to Mom and wait for the afterbirth to come out.

All of it, every bit, has to be brought back to the hospital to be examined—to make sure it's all there. If it isn't, they have to remove it. This material is almost always mixed with excretions that come as a result of all the pushing and strain. It's natural. It's okay.

As far as I am concerned, the umbilical clamp (along with the sterile scissors) is the only useful thing that's packed in the huge maternity bags we carry. There's also a bulb syringe to help aspirate the baby's nose and/or mouth. I guess this would be useful as well.

The bag itself is a Gladstone-type satchel, sterilized and sealed. There's an open one for training back at St. John's. The worst thing about the bag is that the sterile gloves are packed halfway down inside it. This means you have to contaminate everything to get at the gloves.

I have mentioned this a few times at the hospital, hoping to get this packing system changed so the gloves are at the top. It never does any good. But you put the gloves on anyway.

We're zooming down Queens Boulevard, and I have to admit: I'm wide awake and very excited. A maternity is one of the things I've wanted to be able to say to my friends and family that I've experienced working on the ambulance, and now it's about to happen.

Here we are. The cops are upstairs. There must be eight or nine people crammed into this tiny apartment. Is there more than one room. It doesn't seem like it.

Everyone is speaking in Spanish, all at the same time, and much too fast for me but not for Jose. He says they want to know if we're going to take them to St. John's or Elmhurst General. St. John's. Good, they like that. If they're happy, we're happy.

But for the moment, nobody's going anywhere. This baby is ready to be born. The contractions are less than a minute apart, Mom is dilated more than ten centimeters, and now we cannot move her from the small sofa she's on until it's all over.

On go the gloves. With the gloves on, we do look the part, and they seem to have an effect on those present. I feel like they're saying to themselves, Okay, these guys are *the guys* and not some *other guys* who just wandered in here, so…proceed.

It is suffocating in this apartment with everyone crowded around sweating and using up the air. But nobody wants to leave. It's also really dark. There's no light other than a single bulb in the center of the room. Who cares. This is an *event*. A *blessed* event, as they say. And who has the right to complain about anything anyway, when it's the mother who's doing all the work—and feeling every minute of it.

Jose is asking Mom how many other *niños* she has, and it turns out there are *cuatro*. He looks at me and winks. What does that mean. Does it mean he thinks this one should be easy. If he does, why not tell that to Mom. Somehow, I don't think he will.

We're basically just standing by, with Jose occasionally coaching the mother with a few well-timed *empuje*s and *bueno*s. The baby is crowning. And here it comes.

In the blink of an eye, out she pops. A little girl. Nobody has to tickle her feet to get her breathing. She's yowling like a lion cub.

It's a girl *and* it's a freaking fiesta. And why shouldn't it be. This is one of life's legitimate occasions for unrestrained joy. So guess what. I'm joyful, too. I'm loving it, sharing it along with everybody else. They're all cheering at the top of their lungs. Everyone is slapping one another, including me, on the back. I hear the clink of glass. Wine is being offered all around. Well, okay, one glass can't hurt. *Muchas gracias.*

Jose and I are waiting to clamp the cord. He says as soon as that's done, we'll put baby and Mom on the stretcher and zip them both down to St. John's.

Well, that's that.

Everything that is happening now is an anticlimax. Don't misunderstand—it's all good. Actually, terrific. But it has gone off without a bit of trouble, and that's just the way you want it. The way everybody wants it, especially Mom. And Jose, of course. And me, too. I feel so good that it went so well. Hell, I feel *great*.

After all the miserable, heartbreaking, stomach-turning calls I've been on, finally a happy one.

I'm riding in the back with Mom and her new little one and little one's actual papa. Has she picked out a name for her girl. She has. Her name will be Luz. One of my favorite names but one that doesn't literally translate into English. It means *light*, of course, and you can't give a kid a name like Light, unless you're a hippie. Maybe Lucy, but it's not the same. Luz is *Luz*.

So here we are. Luz, born in the dark. Mom, exhausted but happy. Dad, proud as he can be. And Jose, beaming at me like he was *my* father. You want a cure for feeling numb. I think I've just discovered it.

SUPPERTIME

PEOPLE IN NEW York tend to eat supper pretty late compared with the rest of the country. My father gets home from the gas station after 8:00 p.m., and that's when we eat. Most of the people we know eat no earlier than 7:00 p.m. When we lived in Nashville, we found most people eat supper around 5:00 or 6:00 p.m. They also call lunch *dinner,* which I don't understand. What's wrong with *lunch* for lunch.

It's a little after 7:00 p.m., and Jose and I have just acquired a whole large pizza with pepperoni, mushrooms, and anchovies. We actually like anchovies, and we can't be alone in that—they still offer them in every pizzeria in New York. All that stuff about *hold the anchovies* is just an unfair joke, as far as I can tell. The reality is any true pizza aficionado loves and respects those humble, incredibly salty, nasty, greasy little fish. I *think* they're fish.

Can we eat a whole large pizza between the two of us. Watch and learn. No wolves at a fresh wapiti kill eat with more vigor than Jose and I at mealtime. Mealtimes are a race against Central, and we're determined to win. I've heard that some animals have expandable sections in their gut so they can ingest huge volumes of prey, because feedings can be few and far between in the wild. Yeah. We're like *that*. The pizza is disappearing slice after slice as Jose's and my auxiliary stomachs expand accordingly. Wow, that was good. Maybe we should get a couple more slices. Maybe another pie. Not just now, though. We have a call.

It's a possible DOA in Corona, in a private house. Jose and I collect the remains of our pizza kill, dispose of it in the ambulance-yard Dumpster, and head to the address.

Now this is a rare bird for this neck of the woods. It's a three-story private home that looks like it's still a residence for just one family instead of having been carved up into apartments. The door is wide open, but no one's here to meet us. The cops are already upstairs. Of course it's a walk-up. Look what we just ate. It's not only a walk-up, but the stairs are some of the narrowest I've seen and the turns are incredibly tight. How would we get our stretcher up here, I wonder. It's academic tonight, because we don't remove DOAs from private homes. Oh my God, we're finally upstairs.

What a climb. Both my standard and auxiliary carnivore stomachs are ready to do something. Rupture. Violently egest their contents. That would be bad. I have heard anchovy stains are almost impossible to get out.

It's suppertime here, too. There are two adjacent rooms

at the end of this top-floor hallway. To the left it looks like a combination kitchen/dining room. There are four or five people there, all adults, apparently in the middle of their meal. Why this room is on the third floor is anybody's guess.

Everyone seems unusually calm. Nobody's saying much. In the room to the right, a small parlor, I see some feet in striped socks. As I close in, I can see more. It is an elderly man lying on the floor, in blue boxers and a sleeveless Marlon Brando undershirt. He's white as a sheet and no wonder: it looks like every ounce of the blood in his body has flowed out onto the carpeted floor around his head and shoulders.

There is a pistol in his right hand.

I've never seen blood like this. It's not the quantity; it's the color. The color of blood can tell you a lot. Very bright and frothy, it's from the lungs. Dark blood is usually from the gut. Dark and foul smelling is the hallmark of a GI bleeder. Very bright, deep red often means carbon monoxide may have been present near the time of death, the same as with a ruddy postmortem complexion.

This man's blood is almost orange. It looks just like some kind of cream-based bottled pasta sauce and has about the same consistency, because it's congealing. I'm trying to imagine what must have been wrong with him to color his blood this strange and vibrant hue when I realize that Jose, the cops, and I are all standing here just staring at the man. Somebody needs to do something. That would be me. I need to take the information.

Who has the vitals, I ask the nearest cop. Almost before I finish this question, we're joined by what appears to be the designated spokesman of the family. And so their story begins. They are all adult brothers and sisters, and this is their father. He is/was eighty-three and has been very depressed lately because of his diabetes and unspecified heart trouble.

Sir, couldn't you have toughed it out just a little longer and waited for nature to take its course. Nobody wants to wait anymore, I guess. It's that all-American thirst for instant gratification. Or instant gratification's inverse emotion, immediate *relief.* From the unbearable suspense of waiting for the inevitable to happen.

He's so afraid of suffering and dying from his illnesses that he kills himself. I've heard of soldiers doing this before going into combat. I don't imagine the psychology of that is a whole lot different from this.

The gun in his hand looks like a .38-caliber Detective Special, and I'm wondering if he is an ex-cop and this was his backup piece. I guess you could consider this a backup situation. His son continues to fill us in. *Pop was depressed since the holidays.* He doesn't say which holidays. *He got up from dinner and the next thing we know we hear this noise and there he is. He shot himself while we was eating.*

Up to now, we've all been keeping a respectful distance from the deceased. I want to appear a bit more useful and take a closer look, so I move in. No wonder he bled so much. It was an in-and-out wound, right through the temples. No messy exit wound, either. Just two perfectly round holes punched on either side of his head. Very neat.

One of the officers comes over and stands by me. He bends down and picks something up. It's a bullet. Clean as it can be, copper jacketed and slightly bent. *Jesus, this guy's ammo must be as old as he was,* he says to no one in particular. It is so old, it couldn't penetrate the floor or even the carpet after going through his skull. For a brief moment, I'm ashamed to say, I think this spent bullet would make an interesting keepsake. Maybe the cornerstone of a future traveling *museo bizarro.* This cannot be. The bullet is evidence. I can't believe I am thinking the thoughts I'm thinking, sometimes. It's not me. Has to be the job. Let me keep telling myself that.

I'm half crouched, looking over the body. I haven't even touched him to feel for a pulse or check out his pupils. He's still as a stone, all his blood is on the floor, and he has a bullet hole on each side of his head. If that's not dead, somebody tell me what is. I stand up again and move back with the others. Now I will get the rest of the info, and we can leave.

As I write, one of the cops comes over to remove the weapon from the dead man's hand. Then we all jump about a foot (except Jose, who blurts out something filthy in Spanish). The dead man moved. He moved *and* he grunted. He isn't dead. *He is not dead.* This is not possible. That's all of his blood, right there. He's eighty-three. He shot himself in the head. He's been lying there at least a half hour. He cannot *not* be dead.

Holy crap.

My ballpoint goes back in my pocket, and Jose and I wheel around and bolt for the stairs. Jose is clearly vexed. That's not like him at all, but it's to be expected in a situation like this. I'm vexed, too. So we're *both* vexed—but for different reasons. When we reach the ambulance, Jose shares the cause of his vexation with me.

We have a problem. Oh shit. Yes, right. We can't get the aluminum stretcher up there. How are we going to remove him. Jose knows, but he obviously doesn't like it. Penny for your thoughts, Jose.

Apparently, and until now unknown to me, there is an old-fashioned canvas stretcher and poles—*a canvas stretcher and poles*—at the very bottom of our bench seat in the ambulance. This actually sounds kind of cool to me at first, and images of Hemingway and World War I immediately come to mind. Hey, Ernest and I, doing our thing on an ambulance, two teenagers toting a canvas stretcher together.

Here's why Jose is vexed. Not only do we have to remove every last bit of stuff from the bench—bandages, splints, padded ties, maternity bag, sheets, blankets, backboard, straitjackets, et cetera—we then have to dig out the stretcher and poles and assemble them and find the wide nylon straps we're going to need to fasten the former-corpse-now-patient in place, so we can carry him down safely. *Safely.* He's 99.99 percent dead. It's our own safety we're thinking about, to be cold about it.

We start our excavation of the bench. Here's the stretcher at last. Only one pole. No, there's the other pole. We assemble the stretcher fast. Do we have everything. We do: stretcher, straps, and a blanket. Up we go. Not too bad so far. We have to hold the stretcher vertically to negotiate the twisty parts as we ascend. Which, of course, means we'll have to hold it vertically when we descend as well. Except that, going down, it will have a person on it. We have three straps. I wish I had grabbed one more.

All this time, we've been working faster and faster. Is it *possible* to save this man. I don't think so, given the amount of blood he has lost. I'm trying to figure out how he can be alive. Blood loss or no blood loss, he still shot himself in the head, and that's usually pretty fatal.

All I can think of is that the bullet must've passed under his brain rather than through it. The wounds are through the temples, but they're pretty low. That could be it. So his brain is largely unaffected. And given the obviously low velocity of the old ammo, maybe there isn't even that much damage from the shock wave. Much damage other than the blood loss, of course, which is catastrophic. Checking for a pulse. I certainly can't get one. Maybe Jose can. But there really isn't time for that now.

We have him strapped down, under the blanket, very tight. One across the chest and shoulders, one across the waist and hands, and one across the lower legs.

Stretcher in hand, Jose and I and start down the hall. I

always like to go down backward, so I go first. We have to stand the stretcher on end and literally *walk* it on the ends of the handles around the first newel post. Once it's around, I squeeze by and grab the lower handles while Jose holds the top and feeds it into position so we can carry it normally. We repeat this process until we're outside. We get him on board. Jose puts on the siren and lights, I think primarily for the family's benefit.

We've radioed Central to tell them we're 10-20 to EGH with a gunshot wound to the head. We're expecting a bit of attention when we roll in. A bit of attention is exactly what we get. One teeny *bit*. I think they're more surprised to see the canvas stretcher than anything else.

A doctor who looks like a twelve-year-old choirboy comes over to see what we've brought him, accompanied by a nurse who could pass for his mother. He has a slice of pepperoni pizza in one hand and a bottle of cream soda in the other. It's suppertime at Elmhurst General Hospital, too.

I tell them the story between breaths. I'm still winded from the exertion.

Young Dr. Malone is looking at me intently as I debrief him. Chewing deliberately. Waiting for me to compose myself. His impassive gaze tells me he has seen a lot and he's not as green as he looks. *Right*, he says. *Okay. Got it. Put him over there.*

He's pointing with the pointless pizza slice. Pointing at nothing. A blank space, against a dark wall.

What. *What.* Is that it. After all we've been through with this call. Have a little appreciation, Dr. Boy. Put on a little show. Play the game a little. You cannot possibly be that jaded already. You're still just a pup. Don't tell me you see this every day, even here. It's a gunshot wound clear through the head. *And it didn't kill the patient.* Doesn't that pique your interest just a little. This is an *emergency* room. Act like it's a damn emergency. Go through the motions, for God's sake.

For your *own* sake.

I'm staring at him as he walks away, and he must know it, because he turns around and comes back to say something. His face is hard, and he looks different. Much older. This time he's not the shiny boy wonder but a razor-edged street-smart New York City punk. He's right up in my face. His breath is perfumed with pepperoni.

What the fuck do you think we can do for this guy, my friend, he whispers, for me alone to hear. As if I should know better than even to pretend it's not a hopeless case.

Well, of course I know better. I also know better than to bring in something like this at suppertime.

But sometimes, you forget.

ALL IT TAKES

NOBODY'S GETTING OUT of this world alive. We all live with a death sentence, so why not do whatever we want. Because sometimes doing whatever you want goes south but doesn't kill you. That's the problem. Do you really want to live in a coma with a tube down your gullet. Or without the use of your arms or legs. Or your privates. Risk-taking isn't as simple as yes or no. Not as romantic as do or die.

Sometimes you do, and you don't die.

I'm not talking about skydiving or alligator wrestling. Those kinds of pastimes are off the charts in terms of risk, obviously.

But how about motorcycle riding. Motorcycles and scooters are the primary means of transportation for millions of people all over the world. People who don't consider themselves risk-takers at all. They just have to get around. Even so, they get hurt. Even when they're not riding for sport or tearing up the pavement.

123

My father and his brother Ralph were big bikers in their day, right here in Elmhurst. They always shared one monster bike or another. They ultimately worked themselves up to an Indian Chief. Ralph was the real road burner, according to Pop. He could be seen at all hours and in all weather, abusing the asphalt up and down Queens Boulevard. Probably right in front of St. John's, before there was a St. John's. Dad was a little cooler—a little less passionate, I mean—but I know he loved it. Uncle Willy was a big biker, too. Motored up from a Honda 250 to a gorgeous ivory-with-black-pinstriping BMW R69S. Hit a puddle of oil the size of a baseball card, fifty feet in front of a toll booth. Riding low and slow but still badly injured. That was the end of his biker days.

You see a lot of bike accidents working on an ambulance. Lots of DOAs. It is not possible for me to ride along certain stretches of the LIE, just to name one road, without remembering exactly where some of these deaths were. Mostly a stretch from the Maspeth gas tanks to the fairgrounds. Lots of them in that stretch. Most of them just ordinary collisions that turned fatal.

Imagine what it would be like to enter the LIE with your bike at full throttle and slam your head into the tip of a steel I beam on the back of a flatbed semi, so hard it pops off your helmet and your skullcap and scoops out your brain all in one smooth stroke.

Try to picture what one of those cool Euro-style café-racer helmets, the cute little demis, can do to your skull. I don't have to try to picture it because I've seen it: a guy and his girlfriend, both DOA. She was wearing the demi, and it bashed her skull in all the way around the border of the helmet. Three-hundred-sixty-degree fracture. That was on the LIE, just at the Maspeth gas tanks, in the left lane going east.

I actually love riding bikes, the few times I've done it. But I'll never be a biker. It's not just that I'm chicken, which I am, thanks to this job and the brains I was born with. It's that nature has blessed or cursed me with a normal torso and rather short legs. It's very difficult for me to come to a stop gracefully and keep a medium-to-large bike upright.

No possibility of me being a repeat passenger, either, after a heart-stopping ride down the Clearview Expressway on the back of a friend's Norton Atlas. Yes, Bill, that damp warmth on your pants came from me. You should have bought a bike with a longer seat.

Tonight is a perfect night for bikers of all persuasions. Hellions and poseurs alike. Every biker in Queens must be out, riding everything from Vespas to Harleys. And quite a few British bikes out as well, going by the faint but pungent smell of burning oil in the air.

I'm working with Jose. It's getting dark, and we're en route from a lovely dinner at White Castle when we get a radio call, man down. Motorcycle.

The call is literally three minutes from where we are, on

a side street perpendicular to Queens Boulevard, just where it passes under the LIE. At a stop sign. Everyone is very calm and collected. There are two policemen and two big guys with Harleys. Both Harleys are parked neatly parallel and upright, kickstands down. One of the guys is sitting in the street. Did something actually happen here. Something that requires an ambulance. At dinnertime, no less. I know we were finished, but there had been some discussion of dessert.

The Harley guys are normal guys, not greasers. They look like they could be plumbers or cops or firemen, any number of legitimate blue-collar types. In other words, not skells. Just responsible, normal, upright citizens. Upright except for one. At any rate, it's obvious everyone feels quite comfortable and even downright chummy. I feel like any minute somebody is going to whip out a six-pack and offer beers all around.

I hate to break this up, you guys, but can you tell us what's the matter. Of course, but not without a proper preamble.

The guy on the ground is Hank, and Hank has dibs on the story, since he's the injured party. Apparently they were riding along minding their own business, really taking it slow and drinking in the night air. *It's such a nice night,* Hank offers.

No argument from me on that point. And while you're at it, please get to the point, Hank.

We came up to this stop and I bumped Frank's bike from behind. I think I may have busted my ankle. Looks as though he came up behind and to the side and possibly struck his ankle on Frank's exhaust pipe.

I couldn't have been going more than two or three miles an hour, max, says Hank. *It was just a tap. It don't even hurt that much. But I don't think I oughta walk on it, do you.*

No, better not.

I think I oughta get it looked at.

Yes, you should.

In keeping with the casual tempo of the call, I begin to fill out my pink slip from top to bottom. Hank, of Hank and Frank, is alert and quite voluble. I've checked his pulse, and it's slightly elevated but not too bad. His pupils look okay. But obviously, he shouldn't walk.

While I've been writing, Jose has gotten the stretcher out of the bus and is wheeling it over. Just to see what's what, in case we need to splint this up before moving Hank, I want to take a peek at his ankle.

When I lift up his pants cuff to look, his foot falls off.

Not *completely* off. It is held on by the thinnest pedicle. Even so, it is essentially amputated.

There's almost no blood. He's in almost no pain. He has no idea what has happened. Jesus, he wants to know how it looks. What am I supposed to tell him. Who could've thought in a million years that a little bump into another bike would take off his foot. I certainly would have upped the tempo of the proceedings if I'd had the slightest inkling how serious this is.

We're going to have to put a splint on this, Hank. It will take a few minutes.

Is it broken, he asks.

Yes, Hank, it's broken.

Half a truth is better than none, I guess. I admit I am a coward, and I will leave it up to Dr. Patel in the ER to give him the bad news. I hope Hank won't be mad at me for not telling him. In my defense, there's a time and a place for everything, and this is not the time nor the place to tell Hank that his foot is history. You never know what the shock can do.

Hank is a great big, hefty guy. I'll bet he eats his share of steak. I'll bet he smokes. I'll bet he can hold his liquor with the best of them. He's a heart attack waiting for an excuse to happen. I don't need to provide the excuse. He needs to hear the bad news in a place where he can get cardiac treatment if it's needed. Not here at the juncture of the Long Island Expressway and Queens Boulevard.

What a damn shame. Hank hit Frank's bike at walking speed, maybe even slower. A goddamn tap was all it took. And now he's footless for the rest of his life. Well, down to *one* foot. Just like that.

But that's the nature of the risk beast. Sometimes you eat it; sometimes it eats you. I guess it's like Pop always says.

You pay your money and you take your chances.

WHAT FRIENDS ARE FOR

I CANNOT FREAKING believe it's Labor Day weekend. I'm headed back to start junior year next week, thank God.

Ever since I started working on the ambulance, college for me has become like vacation.

My grades have been going to hell since the first semester back at school after starting on St. John's. I am so happy to get away from this job that I just kind of *plotz* when I get to Nashville. I drink a lot. I study little. I can't sleep normal hours. I take almost nothing seriously.

On the other hand, I have Barbara. Beautiful in every sense of the word. And a few really great Nashville friends, and so yes, it is like a real vacation being back at Vanderbilt. An incredible relief. The downside is standing on the precipice of flunking out just about every semester—and since I do not fancy a trip to the Mekong Delta, I do the best I can, considering my depressed, exhausted, perpetually hungover state.

I have also gotten really good at feeling sorry for myself. Poor me. Tough shit.

Anyway, it's a wonderful day today. One of those matchless New York days that presage the best time of the year anywhere on earth—autumn in the Big Apple. The air is crisp and it's in the low seventies and there's a nice breeze. What could go wrong on a day like this. What would have *the nerve* to go wrong on a day like this.

Here's what. A call. Man down in Woodside. It's a rush. I'm on with Eddie all week. Eddie is a law student at Fordham and very smart. He's a nice guy, but he can get a little edgy, so I tread lightly.

He reads a lot—law books, of course. He's going to school full-time while he works on the ambulance full-time. Carrying work and school is heroic, in my book.

This week, Eddie and I are on days, which is unusual for him. Nights sync up better with his studies. He has his nose in a book as we get the call. I really admire his study habits. More than admire. I'm in awe and a little jealous. How does he do it. Maybe I can broach the subject with him one of these days. It will have to be soon, with back-to-school on the horizon.

We're in 433 with the lights on and the siren going. Eddie loves the siren. I can't see why. What a racket, right over our heads. But it's not that far a ride, so what the hell.

We're in a small neighborhood, an enclave, really, very middle class for this area, which translates into upscale compared with other locations in Woodside. It's a private house, in a long row of similar houses, the kind with very narrow driveways between them. My guess is these houses were built no later than the twenties, when the widest cars were around the width of a Model A. The cops are here already.

Where is it.

In the garage.

The garage is all the way down at the end of the driveway. I don't think we can make it with the ambulance—the mirrors are enormous and probably add at least three feet to our width. Eddie agrees. So we park at the curb, haul out the stretcher, and start rolling it down the driveway.

This looks just like our garage at home in Bayside. Has to be the same vintage. It's a wood-frame building with barn doors, and it has seen better days. It needs a new paint job badly, and the walls are buckled out at the bottom in places. Inside, it is jam-packed with power tools, cans of oil and solvents, yard tools, bikes, and other important junk. Again, just like ours.

There are six of us on the scene. Eddie and me, two policemen, the patient, and one other man, who turns out to be the patient's friend and neighbor. The patient is sitting on the concrete floor of the garage. There's blood but not a whole lot. Mr. Neighbor has taken care of that.

The patient's pulse and color are good, but one of his legs is totaled, a complete disaster. It will have to come off. Jesus, it's mostly off already. All they'd have to do is debride it, trim it up, make a flap, and close. I have rarely seen such an injury on a living patient. He's not talking but doesn't seem to be in a whole lot of pain. I'm taking the information on my pink sheet while one of the cops tells us the story he's gotten from Mr. Neighbor.

Apparently, against the admonitions of manufacturers, craftsmen, and machine workers all over the world, our patient thought he would save a few bucks and craft a homemade grindstone—to mount on a high-speed electric bench motor. This is a serious piece of equipment and deserves some real respect. My father has one of these at his gas station, and he respects it very much. None of the stones he uses is homemade.

The problem with a stone that isn't made with material specifically designed for one of these powerful electric motors is that the centrifugal force generated can sometimes cause it to disintegrate explosively, with really dire consequences. It is one of these dire consequences that we're witness to on this beautiful pre-autumn day in Queens.

The cop continues. Apparently Mr. Neighbor was in his yard, about an arm's length away, when the stone blew apart. This was a big stone. A piece the size of a healthy wedge of pie went flying into the patient's leg at a very high speed. Like a piece of stone shrapnel fired from a cannon. This pie wedge smashed the man's thigh to pulp, splintering the femur, tearing apart muscles, and ripping open blood vessels. How it missed the femoral artery is anyone's guess and has to be a minor miracle. If it had not missed this vessel, this man would be DOA now. No question.

Almost immediately after the explosion and impact, Mr. Neighbor sprang into action. He grabbed some electrical cord and fashioned a tourniquet to stop the bleeding. I am looking at the wire—I can hardly see it, it is dug in so deep. Mr. Neighbor has applied it so tightly that it is embedded inches into the crook between the leg and groin. I'm trying to get a finger under it. Can't do it. I try to get a pair of bandage scissors under it. Can't do that, either. I don't think I will try the wire cutters, which are right here in the shop. The wire is in there too deep to get any purchase with something that blunt. Just as well.

No point in taking off the tourniquet anyway. The bleeding has stopped. I mean, it has *really* stopped. There is no circulation whatsoever in this leg. This leg is history. Thank you, Mr. Neighbor.

Mr. Neighbor didn't stop with the tourniquet, though. Oh no. Who knows why people do the things they do. There's no explaining it. In some sort of self-styled First-Aider Frenzy, he decided the stone pie wedge needed pulling out, as they do with all those arrows in the westerns. In doing that, he has avulsed the contents of the patient's thigh. I'm staring at them all now. The contents. This incredible mess he has made.

This well-meaning goddamn dumb-ass meddlesome ignorant son of a bitch.

When Mr. Neighbor pulled out the pie, he pulled out most of the stuff inside the thigh with it. And here it all is—pie wedge, bone shards, blood vessels, fat, tendons, muscles—an alfresco anatomy lesson laid out for our inspection. All lying neatly in the crotch of a soon-to-be amputee, on the concrete floor of a beat-up garage workshop in Woodside.

I'm wondering if this man's leg could have been saved if his neighbor had not intervened. I know there's no way I can know this. What I *do* know for sure is that a couple of tragically dumb guys really screwed up here.

I also know for certain that school starts next week. Hallelujah.

TO ALL A GOOD NIGHT

I CAN REMEMBER the exact night I stopped loving Christmas. I was working with Pop at the gas station, outside pumping gas. It was bitterly cold and windy. I think the wind chill, if not the actual temperature, was in the single digits. It wasn't much warmer inside, but at least there was no wind in there. We worked until after 8:00 p.m. as usual and then went home. I was exhausted and I know he was as well. I was too exhausted to enjoy Christmas, and I haven't felt the same about it since.

I know there are occupations where people have to work on Christmas Eve. And Christmas Day as well. And other sacrosanct holidays. But we didn't have to stay open until 8:00 p.m. to pump gas.

The ambulance business is different, of course. Like the diner signs say: WE NEVER CLOSE.

Since I'm the primary relief guy at St. John's, it didn't take them long to start calling the house during the holidays, knowing I'd probably be there, back from school on Christmas break. By *didn't take them long,* I mean my very first Christmas home after starting the job. Because all the guys want to take as much time off for the holidays as they can, I am in constant demand.

The way I feel about Christmas, it doesn't really matter to me if I work or not. So I work. Christmas Eve, Christmas Day, New Year's Eve, New Year's Day. The days and nights in between. Makes no difference to me.

I'm learning that working in the cold weather is dramatically different from working during the warm months of summer. For one thing, there are generally fewer calls. People aren't out and about as much. There seem to be fewer serious traffic accidents. The cold weather appears to even out people's temperaments. There are fewer assaults, fewer fights, and, I believe, fewer homicides. I'm not sure if statistics will bear this out. I'm just going by observation.

There are more of other kinds of calls. Lots of heart attacks and strokes brought on by shoveling snow. Despite seasonal warnings, year after year. The proud, recalcitrant elderly go outside and shovel and come inside and die. It's a shame people are so stubborn, but who wants to admit they can't do what they used to do.

There are lots of minor accidents. Most of them are fender benders caused by the slippery conditions. One time we had to stop counting at thirty accidents, all on overpasses and cloverleafs up by La Guardia. The ramps had turned to solid ice, and about every fifty feet there was a car that had slid into the guardrail and become immobilized. Miraculously, not a single person was hurt.

How did we manage to negotiate those ramps in a top-heavy ambulance with a manual transmission, numb steering, no snow tires, no four-wheel drive, and not even positraction. Beats the hell out of me. Since coming to work for St. John's, I have been amazed at the driving skills of some of the men I work with—and that is during the summer.

Watching them drive in winter, on high-crowned streets paved with Belgian blocks and glazed with ice, is always an awesome—and sometimes terrifying—experience.

Add to that the eves, when there is generously spiked eggnog hidden away in the ER treatment room, and you have the potential for some invigorating sleigh rides, indeed. But so far there have been no incidents or accidents when I've worked winters. That's usually a desirable thing on an ambulance.

Tonight is the night of Christmas Day, and things are pretty quiet. It's snowing heavily, and I don't expect much action out there, but I may have spoken too soon. We've got a call—it's a man down, struck by a car on the Grand Central Parkway right near La Guardia.

A pedestrian crossing the Grand Central at night on Christmas in a blizzard. *Oh why.*

Possible DOA *and* it's a rush. I cannot understand how it can be both a DOA and a rush at once, but that's the way some of these calls come in. Must be Central's version of me doing the dispatching this evening—the holiday replacement guy.

I'm partnered up with Leroy tonight. I've known him as a customer at Dad's gas station since before I started working at St. John's. I don't ride with Leroy a lot and don't have much of an opinion of him one way or another, except that I'm a little bit afraid of him. He is a giant of a man and strong beyond belief. He has to be the most powerful guy we work with, by a big margin.

Leroy is not real talkative, and it can be very hard to read his moods. Impossible, actually. Maybe there's nothing there to read. He has a look of permanent consternation on his face, like someone who thinks he may have been insulted in some manner but can't quite figure out how. Not really angry; more like pre-angry. Maybe he doesn't have moods. Maybe it's just *mood*. The Leroy Mood.

Think morose Li'l Abner with a Queens accent, and you have a good approximation of Leroy.

Sometimes we ambulance guys get involved in a bit of roughhouse grab-ass out in the yard when things are slow and we're feeling a little zestful. *I wuz a-rasslin' around* with Leroy, and he lifted me up two feet off the ground as if I weighed nothing, as opposed to two hundred eleven pounds. This effectively dissipated my momentary zestiness and was quite sobering. I would never, ever want to get on Leroy's bad side. That is for sure. Less sure is how to know when or if I am doing that. I will always be careful with this man.

But tonight we're in a festive frame of mind—at least I am, as festive as one can be when one hates the holidays and is teamed up with a Grinch like Leroy, driving at heart-stopping speed in blinding snow on the way to a rush DOA. You have to live in the moment, they say. Last night's left-over ER eggnog tastes just as good tonight and has created a nice, warm sensation in the bottom of my stomach, and it feels pretty good.

I have to admit the snow is beautiful, in and of itself—and better than that, it covers up some of the ugliness as we make our way from Elmhurst through Astoria to the Grand Central Parkway.

I guess snow can make almost anything look good, like beautiful icing on a crappy cake. Anything but the roads, that is, when you have to be out driving on them. They are getting worse by the minute, and so is the visibility. I see flashing lights up ahead, barely, and it looks like we've found our DOA.

There is very little traffic as we get out and make our way over to the scene. I'm looking for a victim, and I find him, lying faceup under a blanket. That blanket, in turn, is under a fast-accumulating blanket of snow. He's lying about twenty feet behind the car that took his life. He and the car are both in the right-hand lane. I need to check out the poor guy under the blanket to make sure he's beyond assistance.

There are no vital signs whatsoever. He is very dead. If he had been alive, letting him lie there on the cold, snowy road would have probably finished the job that the car started. No blanket could have kept him from going into shock almost immediately. I hope that wasn't what happened. I have to imagine death was virtually instantaneous, even though it's hard to figure out at a glance exactly what killed him. Just putting it all together, I'd say death was due to being hit by a car going forty to fifty miles per hour on the GCP. That's just my expert opinion. I know Leroy must have an opinion, but he's very private about things like that. Opinions.

The driver is a thirtyish white male. He's understandably shaken up and sitting in his car in the driver's seat sideways with the door open. He wants to tell me what happened, and I'm more than willing to listen, even though the wind is picking up and we really should be moving along.

He's an off-duty cop. He tells me he hasn't had anything to drink, despite the fact that this is Christmas Day. I believe him. There's not a hint of alcohol on his breath. Speaking of his breath, I think he may hyperventilate if he doesn't ease up a bit. He's that upset. *Try to breathe deeply through your mouth. Slow, deep breaths. That's good. Just like that.*

I'll bet he's been called to respond to his share of traffic fatalities. But it's so different when you're in the play and not the audience. He starts speaking, rapidly: *Do you know that a lot of the workers at La Guardia cross over this section of the road as a shortcut to get to work,* he asks me. I actually do know that, but I tell him no. He thinks that's who the victim is. *I almost didn't stop. I thought I hit a cardboard box or something; it didn't feel like nothing. I could hardly see from the snow. I wasn't even going that fast. I didn't know what had happened until I looked in my mirror and saw him come flying down behind me. I must of knocked him clear over my car. I don't know, maybe he died when he hit the ground and the impact didn't do it. Do you think. I stopped as soon as I saw what happened. Oh Christ. Oh Jesus Christ.*

Judging from the almost total lack of damage to his car, I could believe that the impact with the car may not have killed the man under the blanket. Judging from the proximity of the body to the car, I believe the officer stopped as quickly as he said. I'm trying to console him as well as I can by simply telling him the truth and not just what I think he'd like to hear. That it's a blinding snowstorm and nobody would expect a pedestrian to be here and he stopped as soon as he knew what had happened and it's not his fault. But it still happened. Nothing I could say would change that.

We have to take him away now. The victim, that is. Although for a moment there I thought we might have to take the driver if he didn't calm down. It wouldn't be the first time that a driver involved in a fatal accident had a coronary at the scene. And it wouldn't be the first time one of those proved fatal.

Leroy and I are going to lift the dead man by his clothing and put him on the stretcher. Leroy has him by the jacket, and I have him by the pants legs. When we lift him up, both of his legs fall out of his trousers, *thump, thump,* onto the snowy highway.

Both have been neatly amputated in exactly the same spot, right at the knee.

Well, *this* was not caused by the fall. It had to be from the impact with the car. How his legs stayed put in his trousers as he catapulted over the vehicle is anyone's guess. At least we don't have to go hunting for them in the snow. I'm trying to figure out if this sounds callous or not. I hope I never get callous about these things. But you have to be practical; you can't come back without all the pieces, and sometimes it's not that easy to find them.

I quickly put the legs on the stretcher, and we re-cover the body and parts with the blanket. I don't want the cop to see this. He'd know then it was his car that probably killed the man, instead of the impact with the road. I personally can't see how it would make a difference, but I think it would to him. So why let him see this if he doesn't have to.

Why spoil his Christmas any more than it is already.

Poor guy. There won't be a single Christmas for the rest of his life when he won't remember this event. And the victim—he should never have tried to cross the Grand Central on foot, much less in a blinding snowstorm. But still, it's a tragedy that he's dead. Assuming he has a family, this will ruin their Christmases for the rest of their lives, too.

I can't help feeling very sad for these two men and their families, and it's making me feel bad about Christmas all over again, starting to reverse my dim hopefulness that I might grow to love it once more. Not only that, but now I feel guilty about being so sorry for myself for having to work that Christmas Eve at Pop's gas station. What was that, compared with this.

The snow is really coming down now. Very heavy. Just not heavy enough.

THE WORST THING YOU'VE EVER SEEN

IT'S THE START of my third summer at St. John's. Today I'm on with Pete, the boss. Hooray. I'm working days this week and so is he, and because I don't have a car yet, he picks me up at home (we both live in Bayside) and he drives me to work. Pete and Pop conspired to get me the job on St. John's, so Pete thinks I owe him big-time and he never lets me forget it, if not overtly, then by his attitude. I'm frankly surprised he's never asked for some kind of rebate for his beneficence.

Pete is short and squat and has the personality of a perpetually agitated crab, always waving his claws menacingly. It doesn't matter at whom. Pete has a reason to be angry. He once fell into a vat of acid, and he never lets anyone forget it. I guess it scarred him for life. Oddly enough, there are no visible scars.

Pete had a job at an ice cream factory as a young man, and he must have been careless and slipped and fell into the acid on the job. According to Pete, there was a big settle-ment, and even though he doesn't *have to do this,* he works on the ambulance anyway. I certainly think he enjoys being the boss. How he got to be boss is shrouded in myth.

At this point in my rapidly vectoring-downhill premed career, I have taken a fair number of chemistry courses. (They do add up when you take them twice.) I have racked my brain trying to figure out what kinds of vats of acid they'd have in an ice cream factory. I mean, people eat this for pleasure, for God's sake. My family and I enjoy Pete's former employer's brand of ice cream all the time. The only possible acids I can think of that they might use are citric or benzoic acid, and even they shouldn't be in any concentra-tion powerful enough to burn anybody that fell into them. Especially a tough guy like Pete.

Even though I've been on the job a couple of years now and have plenty of calls notched on my metaphorical gun-stock, Pete continues to treat me as the new kid on the block. Of course he would. He's a bully.

Looking at him, in all his radiant sourness, I imagine he was probably bullied as a kid (not to mention abused by that vat of acid), and I think he considers it one of his personal life goals to pass it along, as those who are bullied often do. It's irritating to be spoken to like I'm a rookie idiot, but I can live with it. Nobody really takes him seriously.

Pete has a little game he likes to play because he's a cow-ard, which of course is the flip side of the bully coin. Some of the other guys play this game too, but rarely, and none with more relish than Pete.

The game goes like this. A call will come in that terrifies Pete, who then puts on the grimmest face he can muster. Next, he goes all hard-ass. *Come on, kid, let's go. This is probably gonna be the worst thing you've ever seen.* He's saying this to me right now, in fact.

That's the game. Pete is trying to bolster his own nerve by making me lose mine. I'm trying to look suitably worried, but it's hard, especially since Leroy and Caruso are standing right behind Pete, grinning moronically and making faces.

This is a rush call. We're off to the loading docks of a major national trucking company in Long Island City. Apparently, someone has gone and gotten himself squished. This is a lot of information to get from Central, compared with the usual *man down.* I have to say that Pete may be right in that this could be the worst thing I've ever seen, but I'm not all that apprehensive. I've learned you have to let things unfold in their own way. I'm thinking of the line from *Macbeth, Present fears are less than horrible imaginings,* and how it doesn't pay to have too vivid an imagination in this line of work.

So. Is this guy really splattered all over the place. Did he burst, like jumpers sometimes do. Is his face crushed beyond recognition. Are his guts all hanging out and his splintered bones sticking through his skin. Seen that. How many variations on a theme can there be.

There are countless variations. But only the one theme.

How can there ever be a *worst thing you've ever seen* when you know there will always be something worse than that. I say this to my friends when they ask me that very question, *What's the worst thing you've ever seen.* Everybody has a different Worst Hall of Fame. As far as I'm concerned, every call we get (except most maternities) is a *bad call* by definition. Who calls an ambulance unless something bad has happened in the first place. From that point on, it's simply a matter of degree.

We're riding to the scene in dramatically grim silence, if you don't count the siren screaming ten inches above our heads, courtesy of Pete. (If you think passing sirens are annoying, try sitting under one for a few minutes, or all day long; I'm surprised I can still hear at all.) By *dramatically grim silence,* I mean it's kind of stagy. Not really real. Not for me at least. Right now I'm thinking of a half-dozen White Castles, to tell the truth.

Oh good, we're not the first on the scene. The NYFD is here in force. Large and in charge. Their ambulance is much nicer than ours. For one thing, it's huge and intimidating. And so *red.* They have every light going, even though the vehicle is parked, on private property. We always turn our lights off unless we're in traffic. They have style. I have Pete.

I can see the victim now. He's flat on his back. No gore to speak of, but he's looking very…thin, not to get too technical about it. Like about three inches thin. His entire torso has been compacted by the impact of a multi-ton semi backing up to the loading dock. He must have turned to face the approaching rear of the trailer at the last second, which accounts for his being smushed from front to back, rather than side to side—which is what you'd expect, since he was walking by.

Apparently, the procedure is to back up the truck until a loud *bang* is heard, which tells the driver audibly that good contact has been made between the trailer and the platform. That's what the foreman from the trucking company is telling the cops. I wonder if the driver heard the *bang* this time. I doubt it. I wonder what he *did* hear.

The victim's face is slate blue from anoxia. The truck annihilated his lungs and heart in one shot. Death must have been quick, if not instantaneous, and very, very painful.

There are huge signs posted all over the place that warn—expressly forbid—workers from taking shortcuts by walking behind the trucks. Because they might get squished, of course. And even with all these warnings in plain sight day after day, this poor schmuck rolled the dice and came up short.

This is the kind of death that really pisses me off, because it's so damned unnecessary. We see a lot of this on the ambulance. People either omitting the things they should do to preserve life and limb—or committing the things they shouldn't. How catechismal—sins of omission, sins of commission. People who have seat belts but don't use them. Old people who shovel snow. People who don't take their meds or don't disconnect the main power supply when doing electrical work. People who have a flat on the expressway and stand behind their cars to wave traffic around. The list goes on and on.

The point is that life itself is a fatal condition. And real accidents, over which we have no control, happen every day. So why invite the end of life through simple arrogance, laziness, or denial. People fight like hell to live when they're diagnosed with a lethal disease. Why don't they take simple precautions to stay alive when it takes only the slightest bit of effort to do so—much less a *fight*. I hate that.

I'm standing by, watching the proceedings. I don't know where Pete has gotten off to. Maybe he has realized that this is not *the worst thing I've ever seen* and has slunk off to bullshit with the cops. Fine with me. I'm watching a massive guy do CPR on the man with the three-inch-thick chest, trying not to visualize all the bone fragments being shoved through the victim's heart and lungs, again and again. It occurs to me that if this poor guy wasn't dead to begin with, considering all the broken bones inside, this kind of vigorous CPR would do the job nicely.

Excuse me, but this man is dead. You can stop doing that. This is what I *want* to say, but the CPR giver is in a trance, so I keep my mouth shut. Here comes Pete. *Let's go, kid. We can't hang around here all day, you know,* as if that's something I really would like to do. They're going to wait for the scene

149

to be investigated before they release the body, so we're free to leave anyway.

I can't help feeling bad. I feel bad for the victim, who couldn't take a few seconds to save his own miserable life by following the rules and walking around the trucks to get where he was going in such a damn hurry.

I know. Who can say how much longer he would have lived.

Maybe he would have died tomorrow, brained by a meteorite. All I know is he didn't have to die today, here, like this. It's not about total avoidance, which is not possible; it's about *deferral:* always put off until tomorrow what you can possibly avoid today. Especially your own death.

I also feel bad for the dead guy's family. And the fireman who couldn't revive the victim, even using every bit of his considerable strength and heart.

Most of all, I feel bad for Pete. Sorry, Pete, it's not the worst. But cheer up. There's always next time.

SPARE CHANGE

I FEEL TERRIFIC today, thanks to the wonders of modern pharmacology. Last night I discovered I had about a half-dozen pills remaining in a bottle of Dexamyl left over from senior year in high school. This morning I took one, and I feel wonderful. Energetic. Upbeat. Ready to roll. I wish I could feel this way all the time, especially working on the ambulance.

I started taking Dexamyl to lose weight. Dad grew up best pals with a pharmacist in Elmhurst who gets him basically anything he wants. I remember Mom massaging our gums when we had toothaches, with paregoric from an unmarked brown *quart* bottle, obtained courtesy of Barry the druggist. Pure tincture of opium, just sitting in a kitchen cabinet alongside the baking soda.

Dad asked Barry for some diet pills for me, and Barry responded with a huge bottle of time-release Dexamyl capsules. It wasn't considered a big deal, just a normal good-buddy quid pro quo. Dad kept Barry's Caddy running like a top. Barry kept me running like Jesse Owens.

The effects were astonishing. I got the best grades of my life with little apparent (at least to me) effort. I was performing feats of gymnastics I would never have dreamed possible. I was sprinting on the track like an Olympic hopeful. My weight was holding at one hundred forty. Now, it's well over two hundred. Maybe I should think about getting a refill.

Eddie and I have a call, a woman down, on the sidewalk on Roosevelt Avenue. Okay, let's go. Happy to take the call. Happy about everything today. Happy, happy, happy. I wonder if Eddie is thinking something's wrong with me. Maybe he thinks I've had a little too much coffee. No point telling him I've downed a Barry's Little Helper.

At the scene, there are two policemen and a woman about sixty-five or seventy. She's sitting on the curb, with her legs and feet in the street. Her head is bowed down, and her hands are resting at her sides, palms up, on the sidewalk.

She looks utterly exhausted. Vanquished.

As usual, pedestrians are passing us by as if this were perfectly normal. It's about noon, bright and sunny and not too hot. Nothing seems at all out of the ordinary except for this defeated woman, sitting half in the street.

There doesn't seem to be a thing physically wrong with her. She's a little confused and obviously very sad. Her face is wet with tears, and she has a hurt and startled expression in her eyes. I'm beginning to feel like the Dexamyl I took may have gone stale, sitting in my drawer at home. I'm starting to feel awful. This isn't supposed to happen. Neither was whatever happened to this poor woman.

It's difficult to get her to talk. When she does, she tells us a story that is probably pretty common; you just normally don't see the effects firsthand.

She says she's been put out of the house, out on the street, by her daughter and son-in-law. Just forced from the home she shared with them. It's not clear who owns the home, but it's very clear she cannot return there. She has no luggage. No purse. Nothing but the clothes on her back. How the fuck can a thing like this happen. There has to be a law against it or something. The cops say not. Can't they at least make them give her stuff back. Maybe so, but she won't say who they are or where they live. She's afraid.

I ask the cops what's going to happen to her. They say simply that they don't know.

We can't take her to the hospital because she's not injured or ill. The cops would never take her in for vagrancy. So where the hell does she go. What the hell do we do. What does *she* do. She says she doesn't want to go *anywhere*, and we can't make her. We can't unilaterally decide she's insane and take her to EGH against her will. What cosmic sidewalk crack has she fallen into. And if someone like her can end up lost in a crack like this—tell me who can't.

Most of the time when we see homeless people, they've

been homeless for a while. They've adapted in one way or another to that life. They can survive, for better or worse. Maybe they're outside because they choose that life. Many seem to want to live completely unfettered. Lots of them are substance abusers. Some are castaways, like our woman on the sidewalk. But we never see them at the exact moment they've become homeless. Will this woman have the presence of mind to tap the skills she will need to adapt to her isolation in a city of millions. Like some sort of urban Robinson Crusoe but on an overcrowded island. She'll have to adapt fast. Right now, I don't think she has any idea how to get her next meal.

Eddie takes me aside and asks me how much money I have on me. In an instant, I am so deeply shamed that I can hardly speak. Why didn't I think of this myself. I like to think compassion is my number one goal on this job, even when I can't help in any other way.

Yes, of course. We need to give her money. We need to give her *all* of our money, everything we've got, as if it will do any good in the long run, or even in the midterm.

Eddie pulls fourteen bucks out of his pocket, plus a small handful of change. I have a twenty, being unusually flush today. It's not a lot of money, but it will certainly get her through a day or two, at least as far as food is concerned. She has no place to put the money, so we lay it in her palm and then curl her fingers around it, so it stays put. I hope nobody gets smart and grabs it. It would be so easy.

She has nothing else. Not even a couple of matches, some firewood, and some pemmican to chew on before the wolves eat her up. Right in the middle of Queens, NY, USA. And I thought life in the wild was cruel.

I don't know of any flophouses in this section of Queens, so where she will sleep is anybody's guess. Maybe she won't sleep tonight at all.

I know I won't.

CANDY

STANDING HERE LOOKING down at this boy, I feel like he could be my kid brother, if I had one. If I did have one, I wouldn't want to see him like this. He doesn't look like he could be more than twelve, and I know he has to be older than that. But not by much.

He looks so peaceful here, lying in the grass behind this garage on such a rare June day. His eyes are closed like he just lay down and went to sleep. He doesn't look dead at all. I can't remember the last time we had a DOA whose eyes were closed. I wonder if a cop closed them. Maybe he reminded one of them of *his* kid brother.

The grass must be at least two feet high. I'm amazed somebody saw him here and called 911. He could have been here a long time. In this heat, it wouldn't take long for him to decompose. He's such a good-looking, clean-cut kid. Blond hair. A junior Beach Boy. He should be hanging out on Gilgo Beach instead of lying here dead in Maspeth.

A good-looking kid, for sure. He deserves an open coffin. Screw that. What he *deserves* is to be alive.

Lately when I see something like this, I keep getting the strangest sensation. You know how they say that when you have a near miss your whole life flashes before your eyes. When I see some dead people—and I can't tell who it will be—I see *their* lives flash by. There must be a name for this. I'm seeing them as babies being held by their parents. Playing with toys. Starting school. Going to church. Meeting someone. Having a life and growing old. Well, not in this case. I can't help seeing the wholeness of the life that was. The life had substance. It was real. And then it comes to this, and it's so hard to understand why and what's the point. Even harder to figure out is the point of the question *What's the point.* I know by now that there is no point. I wish I could believe there was. You don't know how much I wish that.

Look at the size of that plastic bag full of what. Looks like Seconal. There must be hundreds of them. Maybe well over a thousand. If he had sold them all on the street, he would have made quite a haul.

He has vomit around his mouth and in his nose. He almost certainly aspirated it and suffocated. I have to assume the obvious, that he took some of his own pills. But having this many, he had to have known how far to go. Even as young as he was, with that many pills, he must've known what he was doing. There's no question he was dealing.

I refuse to believe he OD'd on purpose. Such a good-looking kid. So much ahead of him. Not counting a stay at Spofford. At the very least, I'd have thought he'd be looking forward to scoring some big bucks with all those reds. It had to have been accidental. That's what the cops are saying.

How are they going to explain this to his parents. Your son is dead. By the way, did you know he was a drug dealer. He was dealing barbiturates and it looks like he took some himself and OD'd. Sorry for your loss. Jesus.

They've asked us to remove him to the morgue. We can do that. The detectives have been here awhile and have seen all they came to see, and we don't have any other calls on deck right now. One of the cops gently pries the bag of pills out of the dead boy's hand. I wonder where that will end up. Probably in an evidence locker. Too many eyes on it for it to disappear, although I know it must be tempting.

Eddie and I are taking our positions at the feet and head and getting ready to lift him onto the stretcher. I'm up at the head. Eddie has him by the pants legs, I have him by the sleeves—I don't need to get any vomit on myself today. On three. Lift.

There is a dramatic, very loud gurgling gasp from our patient. Holy *shit*.

This kid is alive and we've been standing around talking. That must be why his eyes were closed so nicely—he really *was* sleeping. Holy shit.

But almost as soon as I hear this gasp, I know what has happened. When we lifted him, some air was forced through his vomit-clogged throat, and for just a second it sounded like he was alive, fighting to breathe.

Is it evil of me to be relieved this boy is truly dead, because I am afraid of making a mistake. If that's true, I don't think I should be doing this much longer. Maybe it's already too late.

DON'T BLINK

THINGS ARE REALLY slow today, thank God. And I don't mean I'm thankful because I'm lazy. When we're slow, it means fewer people out there are dying or getting hurt, and that's a good thing. But life goes on, and we'll soon be busy again, and there's nothing we can do about it.

Jose and I are on the way to a possible DOA in a private home in Woodside. No information other than that.

We arrive on the scene, peaceful and pleasant and leafy on this Sunday morning. Our DOA is in the garage behind a private home. There are a couple of neighbors here with the cops.

The garage door is open. There's an elderly, very thin white male—has to be in his mid- to late eighties at least—sitting on the garage floor between some old chairs and what looks like a wood lathe on a stand. He's wearing a T-shirt and boxer shorts. No telling how long he's been here, but he looks pretty fresh. I would think he's been here overnight. Probably went out into the garage to do *what*—we'll never know what.

The neighbors are telling us they hadn't seen the guy for a few days and went to check on him and found him here. I like hearing things like this, people checking on their neighbors. It doesn't happen enough.

We're going to remove him to the Queens General morgue, since we have no calls backed up and nobody thinks the circumstances are suspicious—*nobody,* meaning the police. Nobody else's opinion counts. We don't have to wait here for the crime-scene guys to give this site the once-over, so we're good to go.

But I'm looking at this man, and something is making me want to check him out one more time. He's white as a sheet, his eyes are partially open, and he's really stiff. But there's the faintest patch of pink on his throat, just below his Adam's apple. Like a faded rose tattoo. It shouldn't be there. Not if he's dead. It should be as white as the rest of his body.

I try for a pulse. Jose comes over. *What,* he says. *Looking for a pulse,* I say. Clearly none at the wrist. None at the neck, either. I rub my finger across his eyes. This is something Eddie taught me and something we never do if family is present, because it looks atrocious.

Eddie says when you're really not sure if somebody's dead you should try drawing a finger across an eyeball and waiting a bit to see if any tears form. Usually the eyes of a corpse will be leathery, with a dull luster. But according to Eddie, if there's still life, tears will form, which is sup-posedly an autonomic reflex. I've never heard this from anybody else, and I'm not sure if it's grounded in any kind of known medical science, but I give it a try. Nothing.

So. Can't get a pulse anywhere. Dry eyes. No obvious respiration. Stiff. But there's that faded rose. And no livor, which would be expected in his lower body. He's pale all over. I point the pink patch out to Jose.

We're both really in close, staring at the man's throat, and one of the cops comes over to see what's up. Then I see what I couldn't feel. The edge of the pink patch is moving—pulsating—so slightly and so slowly that I have to blink and refocus to make sure I'm seeing it. I whisper to Jose. *See that.* He sees it. I turn to the cop.

This guy is still alive. We have to take him in.

I have to qualify that. He is the least alive of anybody I have ever seen. Who knows how long he's been here in this garage. Probably the *few days* that his neighbors haven't seen him. He could have had a stroke or something two or three days ago and just degenerated from that point until today.

Now I'm as annoyed with the neighbors as I was proud of them when we first got here.

If they hadn't seen him around for a while, why didn't they go looking sooner. After one day instead of three. I understand it takes a bit of time before you realize you haven't seen somebody lately. But a guy this old—a friend—they should have dropped in on him daily. We might have been able to save him. Now I don't think we can.

At first, the cops don't believe me, but then they get

agitated. Not angry but busy. We've all been caught by surprise. Jose and I run and get the stretcher. The cops have already lifted him up, and they just plop him on top of the stretcher, and into the ambulance he goes. And we're off to EGH.

We're not making this a rush call, but we're not taking our time, either. Lights but no siren. Jose can drive very quickly when he wants to, but he's so smooth you never think he's speeding—which we're actually not supposed to do, no matter what. It always surprises everyone when I tell them that we're not supposed to violate any traffic laws, even though we're an ambulance. But we do it every day. You just have to be careful.

In the back, I'm sitting on the bench looking at this man. There is absolutely no sign of life except for the rose patch on his throat and the faint pulse on the rose's edge, which seems to be getting fainter. I'm wondering if I'm actually going to see him die.

I'm trying to think if I've ever seen someone die before; seen the exact moment when a life ends. I don't believe I have. You read all kinds of accounts of what happens at the moment of death. People talk about rising up and looking down on themselves. White lights. Visions. But these people haven't died; if they had, they wouldn't come back to talk about it. When you're dead, you're dead.

But that isn't what I'm talking about, what people think they see when they die.

I'm talking about seeing the moment of *another* person's death. I've seen machines indicate the moment— oscilloscopes showing flatlines—but the people showed no physical signs of departing. A machine is a step removed from the reality. It's a phone call instead of a face-to-face conversation.

I'm looking for something that will visibly mark this man's passing on. I want a sign. Anything, really. A wisp of ascending vapor. The corporeal phlogiston of his burned-out soul passing up to heaven. Something mystical and beyond rational explanation.

I'll have to settle for the disappearance of the rose on his throat.

It's not that I'm a voyeur. I just want to be present, to be a witness to his passing. This man has no one but me to do this for him. I've always hated the thought of dying alone. All of us deserve to have someone with us at the end, and I will be there for him.

I guess we're about halfway to Elmhurst General. I'm staring so intently at the man's throat that my vision is starting to blur. Moving my eyes from side to side helps a little. This is like trying to see the sun go down. It moves so slowly that the movement is undetectable, but you know it's going. If you look away for even a split second, it's over.

My eyes are burning and I take them off the rose for half a second.

When I look back, it's gone.

SOMEBODY ELSE'S SHOES

PEOPLE CAN GET violently angry when they're grief-stricken. If you're in their way, you can get hurt.

I think this may be truer in New York than other places in the United States. We New Yorkers tend to be closer to our ethnic roots. You know that joke about what WASP brothers do after not having seen each other for thirty years (exchange business cards).

New Yorkers are not like that.

Of course, I don't want to make generalizations. I'm just going by my family, which yells a lot, and my experiences on the ambulance, where we cover the whole melting pot, including plenty of cultures in which the physical expression of emotions is the norm. But wherever they're from, whatever their cultural heritage, people in New York are well known to express themselves readily and freely.

Things can get biblical. I've seen people cutting themselves, beating their heads against walls, ripping their clothing, scratching their faces, and pulling out their hair.

I've also seen people cutting others who happen to be around, or pounding them, scratching them, grabbing them, and screaming in their faces.

There's an old expression that people usually attribute to the Romans but I understand goes all the way back to ancient Greece: when someone brings you bad news, you kill the messenger. Or shoot the messenger, as the modern version goes. In our family, if I ever went to my father to report bad news, I was the one on the receiving end of his wrath. The point is, especially in an emotionally charged situation and especially in New York: when you have bad news to deliver, you'd be wise to deliver it out of arm's reach.

I myself have been pummeled on the body, grabbed, punched in the face, and had my arm twisted almost to the breaking point. Also kicked, nearly stabbed, scratched with fingernails, bitten, and spit on. What did I do, other than deliver the bad news. I was hapless enough to be too close to the recipient(s). Sometimes, you can't get away.

Jose and I have a call in Kew Gardens. It's a rush; possible DOA. It's a baby. I know Jose is as sick with dread as I am. We're not alone in that. Losing a child is as bad as life gets. For everybody.

It's a very nice building. The cops have left word with the doorman to tell us where to go. Judging from the look on his face, he knows what we're here for.

This happens a lot on calls. Instant group telepathy, or

so it seems. It makes me think of a school of fish, instantly changing directions and moving as one.

People on the scene know the whole story and the back-story and everything in between. You want to know what happened, just ask a bystander.

Oh good Christ. It's a sweet young family. Mom and Dad and two kids in the living room. A beautiful *Life* magazine feature-story family. The mom and dad can't be beyond their late thirties. The kids look to be eight and ten or so. So they probably have an idea what's going on—almost but not for sure. Yet.

I don't want to be here. I *really* do not want to be here, God, please. Well, who would.

One of the cops ushers me down a hall to the baby's room. It's a large apartment, and apparently each child has his or her own room, including the baby. As discreetly as he can, Jose is blocking the door to the room as I go in to examine the infant, who is lying very still in his crib. I say *his* crib: there are blue blankets and cowboys on the wall. I can hear Jose making small talk behind me. He's telling the mother that we're going to check the baby out, and it's better if she waits there for a minute, *Thank you so much, dear—and Dad could you please keep Brother and Sister in the living room for now.*

I'm looking at the baby. The cops are looking at the baby and then back at me as if they expect me to say something other than what I'm going to say, which is that the infant is dead. He's been dead for a while, and he's blue. I guess this is what they call a crib death. No one seems to agree on what that is and, of course, if they can't agree on what it is, they can't offer any suggestions on how to prevent it. More covers/fewer covers. Put them on their backs/put them on their tummies. It just seems to happen, even to healthy babies, without any warning at all.

The baby is ice cold. It's about 8:00 a.m., and I'd say he's been gone for at least a couple of hours, but it could be less. Babies give up their warmth so fast.

I am doing my best to prolong this moment, looking down at the infant, pretending to still be trying to find a pulse or something. *Anything.* Anything to keep from having to turn around and face the family.

I feel like I'm paralyzed. I know the mom is looking at me. I can feel her eyes on my back. I know what she's thinking. She wants me to spin around dramatically and run out to the ambulance with the baby and see us tear off to the hospital with lights blazing and siren wailing. We're going to save your baby.

This is what she wants, but she can't have it.

I have to turn around and face her. Jesus, Jose, why did you let her get right up behind me like this. Her face is only inches from mine. I know she knows. I know she knows what I'm going to say. Why is she going to make me say it.

She could just ask, *Is he,* and I could just say, *Yes.* Or even just nod. Lady, please don't do this to me. Please don't.

She says nothing. I have to say it. I can't think of five words harder to get out of my mouth: *I'm so sorry, he's gone.* That's what we say. *Gone.* Sounds so much better than *dead* and not as strange as *passed.* I'm trying not to move my head from side to side, so the kids don't see. They're looking in from down the hall. Dad is just standing there, numb.

I'm bracing myself for the worst. She's so close to me. Is she going to start pounding my face or my chest. Or scratching. She's on the small side. How much damage could she do. They both look pretty genteel, Mom and Dad. Maybe nothing will happen. Does she know how bad I feel about her baby's death. If she did, would it matter. She's raising her hands. Here it comes.

It's nothing. She's not crying or screaming at me or making a hysterical demonstration. Nothing but calm on her face.

She puts both hands flat on my chest, as gently as if I myself were her baby. I can hardly feel them, the pressure is so light, but I know they're there.

She pauses for a moment, leans in very close, looks right through my eyes, and barely whispers: *What am I supposed to tell the other children. Tell me what.*

Until this moment, I was only wishing one thing: that I could disappear into thin air. Vanish like magic. I was wishing I could be in anybody else's shoes, anybody's anywhere, but mine.

Until now.

EROSION

IT'S POINTLESS TO make up a *best of* (meaning *worst of*) list of the calls I've been on. It's pointless because I know it will constantly be changing as time goes on. There's always something to top the list, looming just over the horizon. And beyond that, something even worse. And on it goes.

Much better to group *worsts* by category. Horrifying injuries. Decomposing bodies. The death or abuse of a child. The lives people lead.

Maybe it seems like that last category shouldn't be up there with the others. It's not really something that generates an adrenaline rush or keeps me up nights. It's more insidious and in a way more disturbing than the others.

After all, accidents and other terrible things happen by chance, at the spur of the moment. It's the slow-simmering degeneration of people's lives that really baffles me. It leaves me wondering how they let themselves get that way and how they never noticed or never cared. Or both.

There are people walking around every day with jobs, driver's licenses, children, and voter-registration cards who are barely conscious they're alive. It's stunning to think they can function in the real world, but they can and do. In many ways, they're almost feral. I imagine they exist the way the cavemen lived. Maybe not as nice as that.

It's hard to say why this is. I'm sure a good number of them are not that intelligent, which isn't their fault. God bless them.

The ones I'm talking about almost certainly went to accredited schools where they would have been exposed at some point to topics like what to eat, how to clean themselves, and where babies come from. Would have been exposed to these things. But maybe they just never sank in.

These are people who seem to have little or no idea of how the human body functions. Who have no concern whatever with hygiene, proper nutrition, or how to take care of themselves, their families, or their living space.

You have to exclude the elderly from this group, even though they represent a lot of the sad cases you run into, where things have slid downhill, past the point of no return.

People get old. They get weak. They stop caring or become unable to care. They can't smell or see things the way they used to. They can't take out the garbage or care for their pets. They don't take their meds or can't get out to buy them. They can't bathe. They get injured and they get infections. It takes a lot of attention to maintain order in old age. I don't think most of us are capable of maintaining this attention all the way to the end, and if we don't have someone looking over our shoulder to help, things can get very bad indeed.

But I'm not talking about the elderly or those who are impaired in some way and can't help themselves.

I'm talking about the man in the back of 434 as we're rolling up Woodhaven Boulevard, who has forced me to stick both my hands out of the window as far as I can, because they stink so bad that I'm just *that* close to heaving. And I may yet.

This man's legs are covered with maggots from his groin to his feet.

What isn't covered with maggots is a suppurating mass of pus from wet gangrene. I've seen it before but never like this. Never so extensive or life threatening. From what I've heard about wet gangrene, this could definitely prove fatal for him. At the very least, he'll probably lose both legs immediately, and then it will be touch-and-go to see if they can keep the tissue death from spreading up through the rest of his body.

And I've smelled gangrene before, too, but never, ever, so repulsively foul. Short of a corpse in the full flower of putrefaction, he has got to be one of the worst stinkers ever. Yes, I know I said I wouldn't make *worst* lists, but this case calls for an exception.

We got the call as a difficulty in breathing, a DIB. I can't figure out why it came across like that unless whoever called had a mordant sense of irony and decided nobody could breathe with that kind of stench in the apartment. I guess his room-mate called, because he was the only other person present when we entered the place. The cops, bless their souls, were keeping a prudent distance down the hall, knowing that we were the ones who'd have to go inside and handle—actually touch with our bare hands—this half-rotted human cut of meat. They only give us gloves for maternities.

Eddie and I could hardly keep from gagging. Trying to hold our breath was useless because nobody can hold it *that* long. Of course, there were the maggots. Thousands of them. And the room was full of their mommy and daddy flies, and other flies hoping to become mommies and dad-dies, looking for a clear place to land in the pus so they could start their future fly families.

This was an unremarkable-looking guy. Nothing out of the ordinary. The guy next door. He was conscious and alert. It wasn't the greatest apartment in the world, but it wasn't the worst. He wasn't at all communicative, but I as-sumed he was diabetic, which is usually the first thing we suspect when we see any tissue death in the feet or legs. So that leaves the big question. How the hell can somebody sit on his ass for what must have been a pretty long period of time and let this happen to his body, without getting help. How could his roommate stand the smell and not call for help before this.

The problem has to have started at his feet and worked its way up. Okay, maybe his foot hygiene wasn't the best. But if he was diabetic and taking insulin, he must have been counseled on proper foot care to prevent exactly what we were seeing.

Didn't he smell something. What happened when the first maggots appeared. You see a lot of denial on this job. But I don't think I've ever seen this much. Does he even suspect he's going to lose those legs or maybe—very likely— more. Like his life.

And then we had to touch him. Eddie and I held a brief executive session. We decided to go into the bedroom and take some sheets and the spread off the bed and wrap his legs in them so we could carry him. We didn't want to use our own sheets and blankets on this if at all possible, for obvious reasons.

We laid him back on the couch where he was sitting. He started to moan a little but not much. I was thinking he was in a lot of pain, but it was not possible to know how bad. Eddie took a corner of the bedspread and used it to cover his hand while lifting the patient's legs up under the heels. I grabbed the rest of the spread and wrapped it around his legs. I imagined the little maggots getting crushed and smothered underneath the heavy spread. Good, you disgusting little fuckers. I hoped their moms and dads were seeing this.

I wrapped the spread completely around his legs and,

without wasting any time at all, wrapped the two bedsheets around as well. Eddie and I took a step back to assess our handiwork. It looked good. Just as we got into position to carry him out, we saw the pus again, running the entire length of his legs. It had soaked through all the wrappings right before our eyes.

Eddie went hunting in the apartment, but all he came up with was a dirty checkered tablecloth from the kitchen. We quickly wrapped that around the guy's legs, but even before we finished, the seepage reappeared.

Now this was serious. Neither Eddie nor I wanted to get our hands in this. Actually, Eddie wouldn't have to, since he was the senior man. It was going to be me. He'd take the shoulders, and I'd get to grab the legs. I headed out to the ambulance for backup supplies.

I picked up two medium-weight wool blankets and four sheets, our entire complement of spares, from under the bench. Eddie and I started wrapping with one of the blankets. Surely this would stem the pus tide. No, it didn't. We used the other blanket. No success. We did one sheet. No luck.

Three sheets later, we had used all the wrappings we could find, and I had to face the fact that I was going to have to touch the pus. Not just touch it. *Grasp* it. Grasp it firmly enough to lift this guy off the couch onto the stretcher.

When I did this, more pus oozed out, as if I were squeezing a sponge. A sponge full of pus. I knew this image would stay with me every time I washed my car or did the dishes.

We finally got him on the stretcher and into the ambulance, and now here we are, every window open, driving
faster than necessary to keep as much air moving through
the ambulance as possible so we don't hurl. I don't know if I
will ever get this smell off my hands. I know for sure I won't
get it off today.

All because somebody just sat there and watched himself
decay. Most of the time, erosion happens so gradually that
it's hard to notice.

Not this time.

SURE FOOLED ME

YOU DON'T GET much time to figure things out when you go on a call. I can see why cops are so cautious and edgy when they respond to any kind of call, not just the obviously dangerous ones. It's the ones that aren't obviously dangerous that often end up going bad. People can fool you.

I was working a twenty-four-hour shift with Fred a few weeks ago when we had a rush call, a rape in the projects in Long Island City. It was a hot night, and it looked like everyone who lived there was out in the street when we arrived. Hundreds of people. There could easily have been a thousand or more.

The complainant was a young black woman, maybe in her twenties. She was sitting in the middle of the sidewalk, leaning against one of the chains strung up to keep people off the nonexistent grass. She was a mess. Somebody had beaten her up badly, and she wanted to go to the hospital. The problem was no cops were at the scene. We needed police, because an apparent crime had been committed. Where were they. I'll tell you where they were. They were g-o-n-e gone. A bystander filled us in.

Supposedly the police *had* been there, and the woman had changed her story and said she was *not* raped after all and did *not* want an ambulance, either, and the cops had taken off like bats out of hell. For whatever reason, nobody ever called Central to tell us not to respond.

There is a lot of *racial unrest* (there's a gutless euphemism for you) going around these days, a lot of fury directed especially at the police, and these guys didn't want to be there in a crowd of a thousand angry black bystanders who might have gotten the wrong idea, like maybe they had talked her out of going so they could ditch. It happens.

So there we were. People were starting to yell at us for not picking her up, and I tried to explain why we needed the cops to be on the scene and we had to call in to get a car to respond. To make matters worse, Fred, Fred of the very *Heart* of Dixie, got on the radio and in his biggest, twangiest, outside voice called Central and asked where the hell the cops were because, in his very words, *We got a bunch here in a pretty ugly mood and we can't take her without the cops so get them back here now, goddamnit.* Jesus *Christ*, Fred.

Everyone in earshot heard only one thing Fred said. *A bunch.* A BUNCH. A BUNCH OF *WHAT.* Only an idiot couldn't fill in the word Fred was thinking.

What the fuck does he mean, a BUNCH, I heard several voices say in unison. I should have been scared, but for some insane reason, I wasn't.

Instead, I tried on my regular-Joe, street-diplomat persona and told all who could hear me that they should ignore this guy—I do that every day. He's just an old fart and that's the way he talks and he doesn't mean it and *We're taking her to EGH right now,* so *Please give me a hand with the stretcher.* (Fred was still waiting for Central to tell him where the cops were and if any were responding.) It worked. I actually believe they thought I was the good guy and Fred was the bad guy, both of which happened to be true, and we were going to do the right thing in spite of good ole Fred, the good ole racist. I swear to God I didn't think we were going to get out of there without at least a beating. Maybe worse. But people can fool you. One of the angry guys in the crowd smiled when I asked him to help me with the stretcher. My friend, if we ever meet again, it would please me no end to purchase you a beer.

All this is still very fresh in my head tonight. I'm back on with Fred after not having worked a shift with him since that hot night in the projects. We never speak much, and tonight we're speaking even less. I'm not sure if he heard me bad-mouth him to the crowd but, really, so what. What I think is I saved his ass and maybe my own as well. He's no fool, and he should know this. Beyond that, let him think what he wants.

Tonight we've got a psycho in Elmhurst, Van Horn

Street, literally right up the hill from my father's gas station. It's about eight in the evening, and it's a wonderful night. Much cooler than it has been. It's delicious out. One of the cops is in the house, and the other is escorting us in. Everything seems pretty low key. I believe we've all been seduced by the beautiful evening.

Inside, a mom and dad are standing in the living room, and their son is sitting on the couch. I'd say the son is about thirty. The parents look very old, like they could be his grandparents. *What's the problem, dear,* I ask Mom. *He don't eat. He don't talk. He's been in Creedmoor and a outpatient at Elmhurst and we want him taken in for observation and to see if maybe they can get him to eat somethin'.* They both look very worried. God, I wonder if they have been dealing with this their whole lives, in one way or another. I feel so sorry for them. And I feel even worse when I take a closer look at the son.

The son is at least six foot six or even taller, and I don't think he weighs much more than one hundred thirty pounds, if that. He looks like the pictures of the guys who were on the Bataan Death March. His nails. Those *nails.* I saw a photo once in a book about carnies, and they had some shots of performers who had let their hair and nails grow grotesquely long. That's what his are like. His hair isn't any longer than your average flower child's. But the nails. Wow. They're all curly and have alternating light and dark growth bands. I wonder if you could tell his age by counting them. No, surely not. He's not a tree. How long would they be if they were straight. Maybe a foot. Maybe longer.

I'm finished getting all the information. Fred has the papers from the psych department, so we're ready to leave. Poor Jimmy—that's our patient's name—he can't get up, he's that weak.

Jimmy, can you walk if we help you, or do you want us to get the stretcher.

Call him Little Jimmy, his mom says.

Really. *Can you walk, Little Jimmy.*

He nods yes.

One of the cops, a guy I've worked with before and am pretty friendly with, takes Little Jimmy by his right arm, and I take the left. We help him get up, very slowly and gently. He feels brittle, like something could break off if we don't handle him right. I don't know if my policeman friend feels as sorry for Jimmy as I do, but I think he probably does. It's easy to forget cops come with all the same feelings as the rest of us.

We've gotten Jimmy up, and we're moving, very slowly, to the living-room door. From there, we'll pass through the kitchen and down some stairs to the street and our ambulance. Then it's not more than a ten-minute drive to EGH, if that.

The doorway into the kitchen is narrow, so my policeman friend lets go of Jimmy's arm so he and I can squeeze through. When he does, Jimmy, in one fluid motion, reaches on top of the fridge to my left and grabs a pair of editor's shears—the kind with the really long blades that people use to cut out newspaper articles—and raises them over his head. Holy shit. Little Jimmy's going to kill me, right here in his mom's kitchen. *Holy shit.*

They say things like this tend to happen in slow motion, and I can tell you, they're right. I see Jimmy's hand go up high and then start down, headed right for where my neck meets my chest. I feel the doorframe against my back. There is no room to back up. I see my cop friend's face, mouth in a perfect circle and eyes to match. I see Jimmy's face. He's grinning. He's looking at me like a kid about to open a present. What could be inside. My aorta, I guess. Lungs.

Somehow I have managed to compress myself against the doorframe, and when the blades come down, he just takes out my left shirt pocket, pen included. He has so little strength that it is an easy job for my now best friend ever in blue to immobilize Jimmy's right arm and wrestle the scissors out of his hand. Then he slams Little Jimmy against the fridge and cuffs him but good.

Little Jimmy. Weak, sad, malnourished Little Jimmy who could barely stand up has almost done me in. In hindsight I probably should have been more careful. But it's like I said.

People can fool you.

OMAHA BEACH

THERE'S A STRETCH of road in Queens that's famous for miles around as a center of illegal street racing: it's a section of the Brooklyn–Queens Connecting Highway, part of I-278. Known simply by us locals as the Connecting Highway.

Drag racers love it because it's sunken down low, and spectators can watch from the walls lining the road above. As a bonus, it's easy for accomplices to block off lanes, and the entrance ramps are long enough for the race to proceed without traffic interfering and before the police can get on the highway and break it up.

The section the street racers use is a relatively straight quarter-mile-plus run. Other sections aren't so straight.

I hate this road, even in the daytime. Even when it's clear and there isn't much traffic, which admittedly is seldom. Now that I have my own car, I'm driving around more, and sometimes, when there's no other way, I find myself on the Connecting Highway, going home to Bay-side from the city.

Right after you get off the Triborough Bridge heading east toward La Guardia, there is a series of really nasty curves. Everybody drives too fast and tailgates through there, and the lanes are extremely narrow, and it always gives me the sweats when I'm driving on it. Today I can see my sweats are not unfounded.

We're here on a rush call. There are multiple automobiles involved in a series of collisions, and there are multiple injuries and DOAs. We're up on the service road because the highway is blocked off by emergency vehicles — mostly fire trucks and police cars. I thought *we* were an emergency vehicle. How are we supposed to get down there to pick up the survivors, assuming there are any. The answer is we can't, at least not with the ambulance. We're going to have to attack on foot.

First things first — have to find a parking place on the service road. Then we have to figure out how to get down there.

I'm on today with a guy we all call Tony. Tony doesn't have a nickname. You have to like somebody to give him a nickname, and nobody really likes Tony. The guy drives anyone who works with him crazy. It only takes about an hour or so before you want to open the ambulance door and jump out at high speed. Which is the speed you're usually going when Tony is at the wheel.

It's not just that he drives too fast, but he drives *jerky*. All his moves are abrupt. He smashes the bus into gear. He pops the clutch. He darts from lane to lane. He flings the ambulance around corners. He waits until the last minute to hit the brakes, and then he slams them on—it feels like he's using both feet on the brake pedal.

This is bad enough when the ambulance is empty, but he does it when we have patients on board.

You can't treat somebody or write down their information when you're being slammed around by Evel Knievel. Patients, the ones who can speak, complain about this, and I've had to yell at Tony and curse him out to slow down. And he will slow down, for about half a minute. Then he's right back on the hot pedal.

Even outside the ambulance, he moves like he's on speed. On top of it all, he's totally oblivious to our criticism. It just rolls right off his back. I'd say he's cheerful, but he's just…busy. Busy, busy, busy. Like a mongoose in pants and a shirt who can drive a stick.

Speaking of pants and a shirt, he's no poster boy for personal hygiene, either. To be blunt, he's a pig. Which is a definite minus when you're working for a hospital. He's a pig with the metabolism of a mongoose. Try to picture that. It's disturbing, right. The reality is worse.

So Tony is just *Tony*, and the only time we call him something else is when it's an expletive.

There's a wall about four feet high and then a steep

grassy slope all the way down to the road. Before we start over the wall, we have a good look at the scene. It looks like pictures of the beach on D-day. There are bodies all over the place. Some are alive; more appear to be dead.

It's hard to tell how many cars are actually smashed up, it's such a mess. It looks like several Checker cabs are involved. Checkers can hold a lot of passengers, and they don't have seat belts. My guess is that when all these cars started smashing into one another, and the Checkers got hit by more cars as they spun around, they probably spit out their fares all over the road and in front of oncoming cars. It's almost certain many of the victims got hit two times. Or more.

This road is in a canyon. There's no place for cars to go but into the walls or the divider and then carom back onto the road, into yet more cars and over more victims. What a road. What a massacre.

Tony lets me go over the wall first. Oh hell, I can hardly stand up. Not only is it quite a slope, but the grass is damp and slippery. It feels like someone sprayed it with oil. But I'm over. Tony wrestles the stretcher over and immediately slips and slides down the wet grass on his butt until he's almost on the road. Going down via butt seems like a good plan, if it can be done slowly, and I sit down carefully and work my way down with one hand on the grass for braking and the other holding the stretcher.

It looks worse from down here than it did from up there.

I don't see anyone who appears alive. We'll have to search for survivors. The injuries are horrible. One in particular has stopped me in my tracks.

I'm standing over a dead man in a business suit. I should say part of a business suit. He has no pants on. They're nowhere in sight. One of his legs is curled around like a pretzel. A very tight pretzel. With the foot at an unnatural angle, resting on his upper thigh.

Every couple of inches, on opposite sides of the leg, from the ankle to above the knee, there are large, sharp edged, V-shaped hunks of leg missing. It's as if an insane surgeon had methodically and precisely made the cuts. I once bought a rubber snake from a novelty store, and it was molded just like this man's leg is cut, in opposing Vs, so it would wiggle in a realistically snaky manner. You poor businessman. I'm sorry you're gone, but I hope you were dead before you could see what became of your leg.

I've lost Tony. Where the hell has he scurried off to now. It's chaos down here. Firemen and cops and ambulance crews are all over the place. Everybody's tripping over fire hoses and trying not to slip on water mixed with oil and foam and glass and gasoline. Lots of gasoline. Something bad—over and above what we're here to deal with—could happen if we're all not very careful. God, all we need is for this scene to light up. It's a mystery why it hasn't already.

Here comes Tony at full twitch. He's waving at me

frantically, the only way he waves, to come with. He's found a live one. There's so much crap on the street I have to lift up the stretcher and carry it by hand, over the car pieces and hoses and bodies and body parts. Tony says this woman is alive. Mind if I check. Good for you, Tony. She's still with us. She's unconscious but definitely alive, though she has severe lacerations and may have spinal or internal injuries, always a possibility. No time to go back up for the backboard, though.

Tony and I are poised to lift her onto the stretcher when two firemen appear and proceed to usurp her berth on the stretcher with a man who is quite obviously dead.

Whoa, whoa, whoa, you guys, this man is dead.

No, he isn't.

Yes, he is. And there they go.

In the heat of the moment, our stretcher has been taken away from a woman who might have made it, to be put into use for the pointless transportation of a dead man. Tony and I have no choice but leave the woman on the ground and try to keep up with the firemen who are slipping and sliding with the stretcher up the grassy hill. Lady, I'm sorry. Please forgive us. Please forgive them. It's all we can do to scramble up the hill and catch up with the firemen at the wall, where they're waiting for us to climb over so they can pass us the stretcher.

I feel sick. I hope to God someone else will pick up the woman and get her to a hospital in time. Maybe they won't be able to save her, but she deserves a shot, at least. At least a shot.

We're supposed to save lives, not operate the River Styx Express. I know it's not our fault. Is it the firemen's. It's not for me to say. They made a command decision, and that's that. They're trained to be decisive under the worst circumstances. Circumstances where you do not get a chance to second-guess yourself. I wouldn't want their job for a million bucks, not that I could do it anyway. They do incredible things. This time, they made a mistake. It happens. It's the Fog of War.

Take it easy, for Christ's sake, Tony, slow down. We don't need to get killed today, too. Slow down, you goddamn little rat bastard. Nothing I am saying to Tony has any effect whatever. It never does.

Now this is too freaking much. Just too much. They're giving us a hard time at Elmhurst General for bringing in a dead man. *Hey, St. John's,* they're telling us, *you got us mixed up with Queens General. This guy goes in the morgue.*

No shit.

I don't know if I have the energy to go through the story. I don't. I'm insisting he's DIT—died in transit. I don't think they believe me. I wouldn't, either. I don't care. He has stopped bleeding for a while, and we all can clearly see that. His lacerations have started to dry out and crust over on the edges.

Maybe we should have taken him to the morgue, but

EGH is closer—and we have to return to the scene. Maybe we'll be able to pick up someone whose life can be saved. Maybe it will be the woman we left in the sun on the pavement on the Connecting Highway. Maybe, maybe, maybe.

Look, we'd love to stay and talk but we have to run.

There's more where he came from.

THE SIGHT OF BLOOD

BLOOD NEVER BOTHERS me much. I know there are those who faint at the sight of it, although I haven't seen that. But I know personally someone who has fainted just hearing it discussed.

Last fall when I got back to Nashville, I was having Sunday brunch at the Burger King across West End Avenue from my dorm with one of my best friends, Dave. He had brought along another guy, named Ry, whom I had never met before, and we three sat down to our Whoppers, large fries, and shakes to discuss our summers and fuel up for the start of classes the next day.

As usual, Dave wanted to hear about my summer working for St. John's. Dave and I are both premeds. He's brilliant, a chemistry major. He's brilliant *and* he actually works hard studying. He will be a doctor. I won't. I could say this job has ruined me for it. I could say I'm psychologically trashed. I could say a lot of things. The truth is I don't want to be around the injured, sick, and dying any more than I can help it. I just don't want that to be my future. It's also true that I have always had terrible study habits. And finally—I'm just not that smart. I believe you have to be uniquely gifted to master organic chemistry, calculus, advanced biology, and physics. Dave is. I'm not.

But ambulance stories have little to do with medicine, after all.

Ambulance stories are campfire tales. They have the power to disgust or frighten or sadden or even exhilarate both the teller and the listeners. In this case, me and Ry and Dave.

I was sitting across from Ry as we were eating, and I happened to be telling a story about a call we had over the summer, a massive accident involving multiple cars and several DOAs. The street was flooded in blood. The blood was deep at the curb. Several inches. So deep that before I knew it, it had washed over the tops of my shoes, soaking my socks and my feet.

Normally we have a change of shirt and pants at the hospital in case we get messy on a call. I don't believe any of us would have ever thought to have another set of shoes and socks to wear. When I got back to St. John's after this call, I squooshed myself through the ER, past wide-eyed patients, into the bathroom, took off my shoes and poured the residual blood into the toilet, wrung out my socks, and dried off everything as well as I could with paper towels, which

I threw without thinking into the toilet. Rather than risk backing up the toilet, I didn't flush. I often wondered what the next guy in there thought had happened.

Despite my best cleanup efforts, my footwear was a bloody, soggy mess for the rest of my shift. Several hours.

While I was recounting this event, I noticed Ry had stopped in midbite. He was holding his Whopper in both hands with his elbows on the table and his mouth partly open, but he wasn't chewing, even though his mouth held an enormous burger bolus.

His face was dead white and brilliant with sweat. For just a moment, I thought he was having a heart attack. He was staring straight at me when he went down, sideways, onto the Burger King floor. Whopper, fries, shake, tray, and all. This was a first for me. I had never seen anyone faint at the sight of blood, but now I'd seen someone faint at the sound of it.

I felt horrible. And yet fascinated at the same time. Ry was fine. It turned out that he also fainted at the sight of hypodermic needles, which I couldn't have known. I apologized and secretly hoped we could still stay friends. And we have.

Blood is fascinating. It has so many forms, from black and viscous to thin and runny. It can be as slippery as oil and then turn sticky. It can congeal like gelatin and then turn dry and crusty. I can't think of any other liquid that has the same complex properties. It also smells peculiar.

I've heard the smell described as metallic, and I think I'd agree with that.

When I was in grammar school, I briefly studied the bugle. I was fascinated by the curious smell my fingers took on after contact with the tarnished brass (it was a used bugle). That's how blood smells to me. Like the smell of brass on fingers.

It can smell a lot worse than that.

Lenny and I were hanging out in the ambulance on a blistering day in the yard, hoping things would stay slow enough to let us catch a catnap. Things were slow enough, but we couldn't sleep. Something smelled funny. So funny that we both decided to check it out.

We went in the back, and it was clean. Not eat-off-the-floor-clean like an operating room, but clean enough. Nothing visibly wrong, but the smell was definitely coming from the back. It smelled really bad, but neither one of us could put a finger on it. We opened the bench. Nothing there. Lenny looked at the floor. There was just the slightest brick-red line of color around the hatch in the floor, under which there's a dry sump where we store all kinds of extra supplies, mainly Kerlix, bandages, gauze, and splints padded with gauze. He and I looked at each other and shrugged, and then I opened the hatch.

Oh my God.

All of our highly absorbent gauzy materials were completely soaked with what looked like gallons of rotting blood. I know it couldn't have been gallons. I'm exaggerating, of course. Max for an adult is around ten pints. Every ounce of which looked like it made its way around the hatch and into the sump to be sucked up by our yards and yards of now-contaminated bandages. It all had to be cleaned out, and it would take a good while to do that.

Lenny and I went inside to call the ambulance out of service and try to find out what happened. We did.

It was a simple story. They had a bleeder overnight. It was dark. They mopped out the ambulance as well as they could without taking it out of service, but of course they had no idea that so much blood—that any, really—had seeped down below the floor. I say *seeped*. It was more like someone had opened up the hatch and squeegeed it all in. It's hard to imagine how much of it was left for them to mop up off the floor. Or how much was left in the poor patient.

It took Lenny and me the better part of two hours in the midafternoon sun to take out the stinking, sopping, blood-drenched materials piece by piece, then soak up the remaining decomposing blood, then wash out the sump by hand and mop the floor and back of the ambulance and let the sump dry out sufficiently to fill it again with new materials. It had to be perfectly dry, or there would be problems. (Employee memo to St. John's: *Install drain in sump.*)

It still didn't bother me all that much, except for that smell.

I've been covered with blood after calls. As I say, I usually have a spare uniform on hand, but sometimes I forget to bring one, so I have come home with blood on my clothes. I always try to hide it from Mom and Dad and my sisters, but once in a while they'll see it and be repulsed. Excuse me, did you guys not know I was working on an ambulance.

It just so happens we're on a rush call right now, and it's a bleeder. Man stabbed. It's about 2:30 on a Sunday morning, and Jose and I both guess there's been some kind of bar brawl or *altercation* (love that euphemism) that led to blood being shed in anger. Could be anything, really.

It's all out in the street. Very theatrical, directly under the ghastly light of a mercury-vapor streetlamp. The cops are here, and there's a kid with a bloody T-shirt wrapped around his right hand. The shirt is soaked, and it must be his, since he's topless. Nobody else is around. He has to be freezing with his shirt off—it's chilly tonight and we don't want to have him going into shock, so we need to be quick about this.

I'm unwrapping the T-shirt and there it is—a deep gash right across his palm from side to side, to the bone. Clearly a defensive wound. He says somebody cut him with a bottle. *It was a broken bottle,* he adds. *Uh-huh,* I say. I figured as much.

He's bleeding heavily, so first order of business is to get that stopped. I hand him a wad of gauze to squeeze and tell him to hold up his arm as high as he can while he's squeezing. The gauze gets soaked quickly, and the bleeding is unabated. Never had a hemophiliac before—could this be my first, I wonder.

I have his elevated arm in my left hand, and I'm starting to bandage his wound with my free hand. *Is that too tight.* He says nothing. Well, too bad anyway, it has to be tight.

While I'm working, a steady stream of his blood is flowing down his arm, over my hand, and onto my bare arm, down to the inside of my elbow. Even though it's chilly, we're wearing our summer short sleeves. And, of course, we never wear gloves except on maternity calls.

Something is a little unsettling. It's his blood. The way it feels.

It feels good. Warm as it is. Running down my hand and arm on this unseasonably cool night. Nice and warm. It feels really good.

God help me. What the hell is happening to me.

DONE

MY PARENTS THOUGHT working on the ambulance at St. John's would be a great job for me as a premed student.

I don't know how to tell them that I think working on an ambulance has turned me against medicine as a career.

Very soon it will be out of my hands anyway, because my grades are just not good enough to get into any decent medical school. To make things worse, I'm burned out. At twenty. Many of the things I've seen, the really awful things that keep me up at night, have nothing remotely to do with the practice of medicine. I've lost my ability to concentrate or take anything seriously. Having almost daily hangovers doesn't help, either.

I'm the first one on either side of the family to go to college. My father is the kind of man de Tocqueville must have had in mind in *Democracy in America* when he wrote about why Americans are more addicted to practical than theoretical science. To my father, college is supposed to teach me a trade.

If I tell him that I no longer think medicine is for me, and that I'm thinking of changing majors from chemistry to English, he'll tell me to pack my bags and come home. To him, a switch to English would be tantamount to giving the finger to the American work ethic. So I am going to finish my premed distribution requirements. Then I'm going to secretly switch majors and the hell with the consequences.

But. *But.* Some things about medicine are still so fascinating to me, not the calculus or the organic chemistry, but the hands-on stuff.

I like it when the surgeons are on duty in the ER. They impress the hell out of me: a surgeon is part healer and part mechanic. They can get rough when they have to. They're not afraid to manhandle. Sometimes they have to pull, shove, and twist parts to get the job done. But other times, they use their hands with a most exquisite precision and finesse.

I've gotten pretty chummy with a couple of the doctors at St. John's, but I particularly like Dr. Kaplan, whom everybody calls Dr. K. He's a plastic surgeon, and I understand he's a really good one, from what everyone says. He's quite round, with a kid's face and rather stubby hands, at least for a surgeon.

Dr. Kaplan has taught me how to suture. Not on a patient, of course, and not your ordinary sutures. He's taught me mattress sutures, the kind plastic surgeons use to keep scarring to a minimum. I can't foresee any situation where

I would use this knowledge without ending up in a court of law, but it's a good party trick back in the dorm. And it's nice to be able to look at a hemostat and see it for what it actually is, instead of a roach clip.

Dr. K. is on tonight, and I can't wait to see how he handles what we've brought him, out of a deep, dark, rain-soaked night on Queens Boulevard.

We've been running all night; there have been accidents all over Queens on account of the pouring rain. It was late, after midnight, and things had finally quieted down, when we got this call.

On the surface, it wasn't a bad accident. A Beetle had rear-ended a truck at a stoplight, a fairly low-speed collision. The only injured parties were in the Beetle, a young guy and his girlfriend. Both of them were about my age—early twenties. He wasn't seriously hurt, but she had a nasty head injury: she had smacked the windshield, and most of the flesh on her forehead was missing, just gone, down to the bone.

While we were fixing her up and getting the information we needed, I noticed her boyfriend had booze breath.

Standard procedure on a call is to make a note when we smell alcohol on a patient's breath—we print a simple *AOB* on our pink sheet. This isn't just for car accidents. Pedestrians get loaded and walk in front of cars and trains. People drink alcohol and take barbiturates—and the ER staff needs to know this. We make these notations for all kinds of reasons. But especially when anesthetics may be needed.

Anyone can have alcohol on their breath after only one drink, so merely noting AOB has no definitive legal meaning. Sometimes we simply don't put it down, like tonight, when we're busy and it's raining and we have to get off the road. Also, the boyfriend went RMA—refused medical aid. Technically, he wasn't our patient at all. So no pink sheet even to write *AOB* on.

We learned at the scene that these two were well known to the police. He was the son of a sergeant at a local precinct. She was the daughter of a captain at another precinct. All very much a family affair. I'm not sure if they were engaged, but it seemed like they might have been or were close to it. It's nice to think of them marrying, uniting two precincts like two kingdoms, a modern-day Henry VIII and Catherine of Aragon.

We got her back to St. John's, and Dr. K. immediately got her prepped in the OR. I say *immediately*—all these things take a little time, after X-rays, et cetera. The films showed no fractures or internal injuries, so she was ready to work on.

Now I am looking on with Dr. K. as he examines our patient's head wound. She is flat on her back on the operating table and the depth of the missing skin, combined with the bleeding that won't stop, is creating a little blood pond on her forehead. Dr. K.'s nurse is sponging up the blood, but as soon as she does, the pond fills back up. Dr. Kaplan appears to be looking for something, but he's not saying anything. Until he says *ha*. I have no idea what he's seeing. Until he shows me.

On the surface of the bloody forehead pond, almost impossible to see, there is a faint ripple in the blood. If you've ever taken a hose into a swimming pool, you've seen something like this. Just a tiny murmur of fluid. A ripple the size of a pinhead. That's what Dr. K. shows me. He's found a bleeder in the pond. But we can't see the blood vessel it's coming from.

Dr. K. says he's going to try to tie off the blood vessel. Not only is it tiny, but invisible under the opaque surface of the blood. This vessel would be hard to see even if it were high and dry. But he's going to have to do this blind.

He selects what has to be the finest diameter of surgical thread available, as far as I know: 10/0. It doesn't look much thicker than spider's silk. I'm watching him watching the ripple. He looks like a bird of prey, an owl, moving his head slightly from side to side, triangulating the source of the ripple—a precise spot that's invisible to the naked eye. He suddenly takes the plunge, his stubby fingers darting in, and, with a few deft movements, ties that little bleeder off. The ripple disappears immediately, and this time when the nurse sponges, the pond doesn't fill up again. It's as impressive as hell.

Unfortunately, it's not the solution to our patient's long-term problem. She is going to require some extensive plastic surgery to replace the large patch of tissue missing from her forehead. With any luck, she'll meet up with Dr. K. again.

I am just about to head into the X-ray room to find a gurney to sleep on when four uniformed policemen march through the doors to the ER, headed right for me. I have the sudden urge to put up my hands, but I don't think they're here to arrest me. All they do is form a semicircle around me and start the third degree:

Did you bring in [her name] *this evening.*

Yes, I did.

Did you notice if there was alcohol on the driver's breath.

Oh hell. So that's what this is about.

This ad hoc tribunal has all the hallmarks of the beginning of a major internecine brouhaha. It's all perfectly clear. The girl is seriously disfigured, and it is going to take some bucks to fix that. The boy is the son of a police *sergeant*. She's the daughter of a police *captain*. From different precincts, no less. So much for uniting the kingdoms.

I did not *notice,* I say, without blinking an eye. And why shouldn't I lie. These guys are putting me on the spot here. In fact, it's *their* job to note if there is AOB, not mine. I'm there to treat the injured and not to collect evidence. My reaction is quick and certain, and I actually think I've put them on the defensive. I'm that pissed.

You know, there were three patrol cars at the scene and you're telling me not one of your guys happened to notice whether the boyfriend had AOB. That seems pretty odd to me.

They know that I know this is going to be a precinct-versus-precinct, sergeant-versus-captain affair. Somebody wants to lay the blame on the boyfriend. It isn't going to be me. I am in no position to say if he was drunk. It was a minor accident that could have happened to anybody. Accidents are happening all over the place tonight. She wasn't wearing a seat belt—and the Beetle had them.

I'm not sure if they're buying the seat-belt part, but I am sure it's not relevant in assigning culpability in this case. I do know that I hate it when people have belts and don't use them. It's not whether or not they'll save your life in a really bad collision. It's about minor fender benders like this one, accidents that can take off your nose or put out an eye or remove half of your teeth or something *minor* like that. Two seconds to snap that belt on might have saved our patient months of pain and suffering.

Talk about extremes. The ecstasy of brilliant medicine and the agony of a down-and-dirty, intercop political street brawl all in one night.

These officers know I'm right. They glare at me for a minute more, and without saying a word, they all turn at once and walk out. We'll see what happens by and by. But for right now, I feel good about having held my ground. I feel great.

Tomorrow I'm telling Dad I'm done with premed.

PAPERWORK

MY TENNESSEE GRANDMOTHER, Jessie, used to tell us spooky stories about all kinds of things, particularly insane people. She is not far removed from her Scots-Irish story-telling roots. She can tell a tale. The neighborhood where she lives, where my grandfather Pee Paw, a retired railroad man, built the house she lives in, is in an area of Nashville known as Sylvan Park. Visiting her in the fifties, via a railroad pass courtesy of Pee Paw, was always an adventure. You got on a sleeper train in the old Penn Station and traveled in comfort all the way. Looking out the window day or night, you saw…nothing. Nothing but fields by day and stars by night.

Once in a while an anonymous hamlet would pass by in a blur. I wondered who lived there and what they might be up to. Especially late at night, in the pallid wash of old-fashioned streetlamps. In the morning there were pancakes in the dining car. As the years went by, we had to change trains more and more, until it was faster and easier just to go by car to visit Tennessee.

Sylvan Park in those days was a time capsule of the late nineteenth and early twentieth centuries. There were no sidewalks. Dogs ran loose in packs. People used fifteen-watt light bulbs; it was very dark at night. They burned their own trash in incinerators built in alleys that ran behind the houses. What they couldn't burn was picked up by trashmen using a horse and wagon. There were railroad tracks not too far from Grandma's house. There were genuine hobos. There was a lot of superstition and dread.

People could *git* you if you weren't careful. Or even if you were.

The hobos could *git* you. Somebody in the alley could *git* you. A maniac could *git* you. It seemed like just about *any-thing* could *git* you. And I admit that considering Grandma's background, at least, she had some right to be paranoid about life. She was the eldest of nine children, and their beloved baby brother had died at seven from tetanus—*lockjaw*—caused by: a rusty nail. If something like a rusty nail can *git* you, you ain't safe *nohow*.

Every night on the front-porch gliders, there were stories of death, sin, and retribution. The sin and retribution tales didn't bother me that much, because I figured those people got what was coming to them. It was the stories about innocent kids waylaid in the bushes by crazy people that got my attention.

Grandma and her neighbors and my mother all agreed that crazy people are endowed with the strength of seven men. Not one more or less. It was always seven. They seemed very sure about this number, and when I would ask how that could be true and, if it were true, how it was determined, they always slid past the question with a simple *It's a well-known fact,* and that was that. They also all agreed that crazy people are completely impervious to pain.

These front-porch stories permanently embedded two things about the insane in my mind. One, they could *git* you at any time, since you'd never know who they were until it was too late. And two, once they had you, they could crush you like a weevil.

I don't think this one could, though.

We're on a psycho call in Elmhurst. The patient is a petite, dazzlingly pretty young woman just a couple of years older than I am. We're in a two-family house, up on the second floor, which is her family's apartment. There are seven people crowded on the landing just outside the kitchen. I'm on with Eddie, and there are two police officers present.

The mom and dad have paperwork on their daughter. She has been under inpatient treatment for schizophrenia. I think they give that diagnosis a lot when they can't figure out what's really wrong. She hasn't been taking her meds, and she's been acting up, they say. They want us to take her to EGH.

She doesn't want to go.

So far, it's a pretty meat-and-potatoes scenario. Usually these situations come to a head with the patient handcuffed to the stretcher until we have time to do a tie-down with our soft, padded restraints, so everything looks kosher. We're not supposed to use handcuffs, which makes sense in theory, but when you have to immobilize someone fast, cuffs are the only way. We borrow them from the cops. A couple of the guys I ride with carry their own, but it's frowned upon, if not actually illegal.

We have other things, too, like straitjackets. My partners and I have screwed around with them a couple times in the yard, trying to see how difficult it would be to actually put one on a person. Three words for that: *forget about it,* even if the person is totally sane and actually cooperating.

Suddenly I'm getting the feeling this call is not going to be as meat-and-potatoes as I thought. I'm looking at this girl. She's not ranting incoherently or talking to herself or tearing out tufts of hair or trying to hurt anyone or doing any of the really obvious things the insane are thought of as doing when they're symptomatic. She looks incredibly pissed off, but she sure doesn't look crazy. I can hear Grandma saying, Well, that's the thing, when you're dealing with maniacs, isn't it.

So what happened. Did this girl sass Mom and Dad one too many times, and they're using their get-into-jail-free card. Did she break curfew. Not do her chores. Date the wrong guy. Or girl. Something isn't right here. She's not causing any kind of disturbance that would normally trigger intervention. It looks a lot like the folks simply want her out of the house. But every last line of the paperwork is in order. We don't have a choice *but* to take her.

It's like an oven in here, and we've been busting our humps all day. My eyes are stinging with sweat. We're all soaked. The humidity has to be close to 100 percent. *Dear, can you please come with us.*

Fuck you. Fuck you, you fucking bastards.

Pissed off is not the same as crazy, but when there are papers that say you're crazy, it doesn't matter.

We're positioning ourselves to take her arms, Eddie and I. She's not a big person. Maybe five foot six and one hundred twenty. As Eddie takes one arm with both hands and I take the other, she turns into a rod of solid titanium. Absolutely rigid. With rage. It's uncanny. Eddie and I have carried some really heavy people in our time, but she seems to have planted herself into the floor somehow. We can't bend her or flex her, and we don't want to manhandle her, at least not yet. One of the cops comes over to help, then the other.

As soon as the cops put their hands on her, she goes totally bananas. She has an incredible grip, and she manages to use it to grab everything within reach. A pot off the stove. A kitchen chair. The doorframe. Half a handlebar mustache, provided by one of New York's Finest. Oh Jesus, is she a fighter. Moments like this are the reason they give us clip-on ties.

She's kicking. She's arching her back. She's twisting. She's absolutely silent all the while, with her teeth tightly clenched. Our hands are sweaty. She's sweaty, too. We can't get a good grip. We can't get her on the stretcher. We're in horribly close quarters and literally holding her right over the stretcher, but we can't seem to get her down *on* the damned thing.

I'm on the edge of collapse, and I'm wondering if we should ask the cops if they can call for EMS or at least another car. The cops are so busy trying to wrangle her they can't even get their cuffs ready, much less on her. One of them looks at Eddie and then back over his shoulder at the cuffs on his belt. He's nodding his head toward the cuffs. He wants Eddie to get them off his belt.

I can see this, too, and I shift my grip so Eddie can grab the cuffs. When she sees them, she goes ballistic. I thought she was strong before. Now it's like someone has plugged her in. While all this is going on, Mom and Dad are just standing in the kitchen with blank expressions. Sorry to be keeping you from your coffee and Danish, you guys. Be patient. We'll get your problem child out of here soon enough.

I'm starting to think maybe Grandma's *strength of seven men* thing has some merit. I know for a fact that this girl has the strength of *at least* four—and really more than that, because she's clearly winning. Doesn't matter. It's not a fair fight. The cuffs never lose.

As soon as Eddie hands the cuffs off to their owner, the officer gets one arm immobilized. Then with two men on her other arm and one on her legs, we get the other flailing limbs hooked up to the aluminum structure of the stretcher. She's yanking the cuffs like crazy against the stretcher, but she's on it and she's not going anywhere. Except, of course, to a mental hospital.

I feel really bad for her. She's completely powerless in all this. Is she condemned for life to be at the mercy of the paperwork. I hope not.

I wish I could be out on the porch with Grandma and her circle of doom right now. I have something else for them to worry about *gittin'* them. Something far worse than mere maniacs.

It's called paperwork.

That paperwork will git you every time.

TWO PRISONERS

I'M HAVING TROUBLE visualizing ever not working on this damned ambulance. I started this job the summer after freshman year. I've been here every summer since. And winter vacations. Now I'm twenty-one, it's three months since graduation, and I'm still here. I'm stuck. I enlisted in the New York Army National Guard a few weeks ago. I have no idea when they're going to send me to basic training. That will mean another six months in suspended animation.

Fred and I aren't speaking even though we're working together a lot these days. We have nothing to say to each other. Then again, we never did speak all that much. It seems like I've known him all my life.

Each call is like a dream now. I have all the moves, the script, the techniques, down pat. Have I seen it all yet. Not even close, I'm sure of that. Am I interested in what the next bad one might be. Not on your life. I am dead from the neck up. It only took three years. I wonder how long it took Fred. It's hard to imagine him ever not being burned out. I

212

don't think it's possible for either of us to summon anything remotely resembling a normal human emotion. Whatever that is.

Right now we're going on a call to La Guardia. Last time I was here on a call we had to haul a screaming businessman off a plane. *Kidney stones,* he told me, between shrieks. That was last year. Or maybe the year before.

This call came in as a man down, possible overdose. We'll be more or less a taxi on this run. La Guardia is full of cops and medical types, and I bet they're all over this already. Well, how nice; they saved us a parking spot at the terminal. Fred and I get the stretcher and go on inside with one of the cops who's been waiting for us.

He takes us to what looks like some kind of holding room, very bare. There's a stretcher already in here with a man on it. A black male about thirty-five. He's out cold but alive. His pupils are just a little bigger than poppy seeds. *Bet you ten bucks it's heroin, Fred.* Fred just grunts. Of course it is. I'm just trying to get a rise out of him, I guess. I'm that desperate for entertainment. He and I *both* grunt as we heft Sleeping Beauty off of the airport's stretcher and onto ours for the trip to Elmhurst General. We don't bring cases like this back to St. John's—overdosed prisoners, that is. For some reason, they don't like it.

Well, no shit.

Before we start rolling, one of the cops bends down and cuffs our patient to the stretcher; both hands to the side

213

rails. Two pairs of cuffs. He turns to look at me. *This is a very bad boy, you know. He's been drinking his own lemonade.*

He's a dealer and he's been sampling his own product. *This guy was really holding,* says the man in blue. *Three keys, imported from Motor City. Like we don't have enough on the street here.* I'm too tired to do anything but nod. He's obviously trying to impress me with hip cop jargon, but I stopped being impressionable a couple of thousand calls ago.

This cop is the designated hitter to escort us and the prisoner to the hospital. In the back of the moving ambulance, he undergoes a sea change in personality. His cocky affability has turned to ice. He's staring at me. Sizing me up. I have no idea why.

When he starts to undress our patient, I sit up straight. Now you have my complete attention, Officer, that's for sure. Not only that, but the guy on the stretcher has on some underwear I've never seen before and I'm sure I'll never forget.

Picture long johns. One-piece long johns made of bright red nylon. With short sleeves and short legs and white buttons all the way down the front. I guess you'd call them *short* johns. Really quite jaunty but not for me. Our police escort is searching the patient, which seems normal enough. He's being very thorough. Maybe more thorough than he needs to be. When he starts unbuttoning the short johns, my mouth opens, but I don't say anything. The cop sees this and gives me another one of those looks. He doesn't have to say *shut up,* but that's what I'm hearing.

He's pulling something out of the guy's underwear, something long and flexible. For a split second, backlit against the bright light coming through the window, it looks like he's removing a length of the guy's intestines. But it's not intestines. It's a very long, thick, flexible money belt. It's red nylon, too. I wonder if it was part of an ensemble, with the underwear.

Fred knows something is up. I can see his beady eyes in the rearview mirror. He keeps looking back. For God's sake, Fred, don't let's crash the stupid ambulance. I know the fact that he can't see is making him very agitated: he always puts both hands at twelve o'clock on the wheel when he's agitated. Now they're not only at twelve, they're actually overlapping. Take it easy, ole Fred.

The cop looks at me intently now. He knows I know this belt is full of cash. Lots and lots of cash. My guess: many thousands. I know why the cop is boring holes in my head. These are the days of the notorious and dreaded Knapp Commission. Internal Affairs is everywhere. Every cop on the street is paranoid, even the 100 percent honest ones. And there are plenty of honest cops out there, no matter what the Knapp Commission says.

However, this particular cop has a good reason to be looking over his shoulder besides the Knapp Commission. It's me. I'm a witness.

And he's a crook.

He's in the process of committing a major felony, good for significant time in the penitentiary. Maybe decades.

A man might do a lot of things to keep from going to prison. Right now, I'm trying my best not to think of what some of those things might be.

You know he ain't gonna need this where he's going, he says flatly, gently patting the money belt. At first I think he means the hospital, but of course he means Rikers Island and then probably Sing Sing. I don't say anything.

Fred is scootching up in his seat as high as he can to get a better angle in the rearview mirror, but he still can't see anything. The moves he's performing would normally make me laugh out loud.

But I can't laugh just now. I'm paralyzed. Officer Dillinger has locked eyes with me. I can't look at Fred or anywhere else. I can hear the crinkle of new money. Without taking his eyes from mine, the man in blue puts something papery and crisp in my hand and leans in very close. *You want a tip, don't you.* It is not a question and does not require an answer. I take the paper and put it into my pocket. I hope Fred hasn't seen. I don't see how he could have.

As we approach Elmhurst General, the tension eases up a bit. It's a relief for things to get back to routine. We drop off our patient and go on our way. I never give the cop a second look. To be honest, I don't have the stones.

Fred is still agitated on the way back to St. John's, judging from his grip on the wheel. Fred is nothing if not direct. *What did that cop say to you back there.* I don't think he has any idea about what just happened.

I don't know, something about this guy was going away for a long time, I say. It's not like Fred to be this easy, but for some reason, he lets it go. From now on, this episode will be between me, myself, and I.

I've locked myself into a stall in the men's room at St. John's. I haven't dared to look in my pocket, to see what I put there in the ambulance, until right this minute. I reach in. I can feel the crisp new bill and gingerly separate it from the tired old soft money in my pocket—all four bucks of it. I pull out the new bill and look at it. Oh for God's sake.

I have just undergone nearly intolerable personal stress and laid my integrity on the line, albeit under duress, for twenty bucks.

What an asshole, that cop. He's much worse than a thief.

He's a lousy tipper.

A VISIT FROM A FRIEND

IT'S THE SUMMER of 1970, and I'm damn lucky to have gotten into the New York Army National Guard, especially considering my low number in the first draft lottery. As soon as I got home after graduation, I called the Army Reserve at Fort Totten, and while they didn't exactly say they weren't accepting recruits, they did say they only talked to prospects between 8:00 a.m. and 8:30 a.m. Mondays and Fridays. Okay. No need to draw me a picture.

One of our neighbors told my parents that because the New York Army National Guard had been federalized the year before to deliver mail during a postal strike, there were openings. The troops who were federalized got a year knocked off their six-year obligation. I went to the Flushing Armory, got an orientation, and the next week I was sworn in.

While I'm waiting to go for basic training, I get to spend drill time at the Flushing Armory mopping floors and cleaning up. Any day now I'll get sent away for six months' active duty, and I still won't have a job when I get out. I suppose I could go back to work on the ambulance, but I know that's not what four years at Vanderbilt were for. On the other hand, I couldn't tell you what they *were* for.

Even so, it's all better than having your shit blown away in some festering jungle in Southeast Asia for absolutely no reason. I have a bunch of friends who went—and are still going—and some who won't be coming back. I have other friends who see no solution other than violent revolution.

I hope when it's over we can all still be on speaking terms. Those of us who are still alive and not in prison or in hiding, that is.

I have lost touch with virtually all of my New York friends by now. Most of the time I work at night and try to sleep by day. I rarely have the opportunity for any kind of social interaction. Make that almost *never.*

But it's not just the job that's created distance between me and the old gang. A few of my closer high-school friends have gotten involved in the New Left—the Students for a Democratic Society. They had been flirting with the SDS in high school, but I thought they'd have grown out of that by now. In the early college days, the few times I did see them, normal conversation became increasingly difficult. I wanted to talk about beer and Barbara. They wanted to talk about Ho Chi Minh and Marx. I wanted to get wasted and forget what I was seeing all week long. They wanted to engage in endless dialectic.

The struggles of everyday existence were more than

enough for me to deal with; fuck the vanguard of the prole-
tariat. You want to talk about a classless society, come with me
for a ride on the ambulance and see how democratic death is.

I did make a few good friends at Vanderbilt, and I've
been to visit one recently. He lives out in the sticks west
of Baltimore and wants to visit New York, so I've invited
him up. I say *lives out in the sticks.* What I mean is that his
family resides in an eighteenth-century estate house, filled
with eighteenth-century art and artifacts, commanding an
eighteenth-century view: you can see nothing but family
land from the house.

The grassy hills surrounding the house roll away to woods
and sky, and the only sound is the faint hum of the faraway
interstate. His family is distantly related to Johns Hopkins,
making him some kind of x-times-removed cousin or
nephew, I think, since Johns had no children of his own. My
friend goes by the name Speed, which at first I thought had
something to do with amphetamines but later found out was
the surname of yet another venerable forebear.

Having seen firsthand how the other half lives, I can say
without qualification that I prefer the Hopkins half.

I have a ride-along on the ambulance planned for him,
so he can see for himself the basis of some of the tales I've
been telling my inner circle every autumn at school, tales
that have earned me the dubious nom de guerre Morgue
Man. This way, he can tell our mutual friends and acquain-
tances that I haven't just been making it all up.

There are seats for only two up front in the ambulance, so it's Jose and me in front and Speed sitting on the front edge of the bench in the back. We're driving around, but we're not on a call—we're actually on our way to get something cold and sweet from the Lemon Ice King of Corona. My new and unexpected favorite: the rum raisin. I'm laying off the lemon for a while; I suspect it's starting to take the enamel off my teeth.

It has been an unusually slow night so far, and I'm getting a little concerned that we won't see any of the action that I've led Speed to believe was a nightly, if not hourly, part of the job. Not that I would ever wish anyone to get hurt or maimed or die for the mere titillation of a friend. I merely want to provide some evidence of my secret life. A little backup testimony.

I'm almost on the verge of making some kind of apology to Speed when we get a call. Woman down. No rush. It's in a private house. Second floor. Over and out and off we go. See you later, Lemon Ice King.

When we get to the house, a man who I assume is the husband is there to greet us and lead us up. No hurry, no panic. No big deal so far. Speed is staying in the ambulance, keeping a low profile. I'm not sure if we're allowed to take friends for ride-alongs, but I'm way past the point of caring enough to ask. If someone at the scene should ask, I'm going to tell them Speed is starting work in a week and this is part of his orientation. In fact, that's just what Pete did when I was starting. Nobody cared then, so why would they now.

There are four of us going up to the second floor. The husband, Jose, a cop, and myself. The other cop is upstairs with the patient, in her bedroom. She's sitting on her bed, and tears are streaming down her face, but it isn't the tears that I notice first.

She is without a doubt the fattest human being I have ever seen.

Sitting *sideways* on her bed with her legs hanging down, she occupies nearly its entire length. She's looking right at us. At me. She seems like a very nice woman, and I'm trying my best not to stare like a kid at a sideshow, but, Holy Jesus, she's enormous. I wouldn't even begin to guess her weight. More than four hundred for sure. Maybe more than five hundred. I think the heaviest person we've ever carried was between three hundred and four hundred. I'm staring for a very practical reason. We need to figure out how to move her, and it won't be easy.

She knows what we're thinking, and before anyone can speak she attempts to lighten the mood by trying a weak laugh and saying through her tears, *You boys will never get me out of here. Last time it took eight big guys.* I believe it.

Our efforts to move her are going to be complicated by the pain she's in. She's diabetic, and both of her legs are gangrenous below the knees, and she must be in nearly intolerable pain. Any attempt to handle her legs—which will be inevitable—is going increase her pain dramatically.

She definitely needs to go to the hospital, and we're going

to take her. The question is not whether, but how. We all re-treat downstairs to make a plan.

Any removal by stretcher or folding chair is completely out. She simply won't fit either one. We're doubtful that we can even get her down the staircase. She's wider than the distance from the wall to the banister, but there has to be some flexibility on her sides, so we may be able to squeeze her through. I wonder how they got her out last time. Has she gained weight since then. Probably so. Pointless questions. This is what it is, right now.

One of the cops has an idea. Since we need reinforcements anyway, he'll call EMS. They'll give us the extra muscle we need, and they may have a few tricks up their sleeve that we don't. While we're waiting, I go back down to the bus to see how Speed is doing. I explain to him that this is the largest person we've ever tried to move and we are waiting for the cavalry to give us some extra carrying power. I have to turn down his offer of help, since he's not insured—in case she falls and gets injured or falls and injures one of us.

While I'm hanging out with Speed and Jose, I size up the interior of the ambulance. Oh Christ, she's not going to fit in here. Not with the stretcher in place. She will easily take up the entire floor of the ambulance, a good-sized Suburban-based vehicle. She may not even make it in between the ambulance wall and the bench seat. Or she may—just.

Once we've gotten her downstairs, we'll be at the point of no return; we'll never be able to put her back. Not all the king's horses nor all the king's men. She will *have to* fit. We'll need to leave the stretcher at the house and return for it, which is something we've never done. We can do that if her husband stays home and doesn't go with her to the hospital. Come to think of it, he can't go to the hospital with her, at least with us. She'll take up the entire rear of the ambulance, and Speed will have to squeeze between me and Jose for the trip. EMS is here.

We all go upstairs to take another look and review the situation. The EMS cops immediately come up with part A of the solution. We'll lay her on a body bag and slide her down the stairs, three of us at the top, two at the bottom, and one holding on to the edge of the bag and walking down the steps, *outside* the banister. *Will this work, you guys.* They're confident it will. What's part B of the solution. We'll cross that bridge when we come to it, I guess.

I've never seen a body bag like the one they've just brought in. It's more like a tarp than a bag: a huge, square, heavy dark green canvas, with loop handles and ties along the side. It looks like a piece of military bivouac equipment. Also, it's dirty. I know these are meant for dead people, but our patient is very much alive. *Do they ever clean these things,* I ask. *Yeah, they clean them, but they can't get the stains out.* Wonderful.

The plan is to spread out the bag on the floor by her bed and then ease her onto it. Sounds straightforward enough, but these things never work out as well as you hope.

The body bag/tarp is all laid out with the bottom end

pointing at the bedroom door toward the stairs. *Can you stand up for us, ma'am.* Yes, she can. We help her up, but immediately she seems like she's about to go over. She is imponderably ponderous. None of us could stop her if she started to go down. We are lumberjacks wondering which way our tree will fall.

Jose and I steady her in front. Her huge, pillowy arms are lying on our shoulders. We turn her slightly so her back is away from the bed, and three of the cops can get behind her and work her down to the tarp. As her back lowers, sliding against the bed frame, Jose and I straighten out her legs, and she starts to shriek. I'm so sorry, lady. It has to be done.

Now she's on the tarp. So much for the two-at-the-bottom theory—it will take more than two to drag the tarp to the top of the stairs. Change in plans. Three of us will pull her down (since that's all that will fit on the stairs), two will take the top, and the sixth man will go down outside the banister as planned. We start to pull. Nothing happens. We pull some more, and still she doesn't budge. Now I'm thinking maybe she's more than five hundred pounds, although the friction from the canvas against the carpeting isn't helping any. We should have put something down first—waxed paper maybe. Too late for that now.

We decide to use short tugs, and those seem to work better. Basically, it's all on the three of us at the bottom, since the guys at the top are really not in a position to help much—they'd have to push, and you can't push a tarp.

We barely get her through the door onto the landing. The stairs are fully carpeted with a thick runner. This is not going to go well. Jose has an idea and asks us all to wait. He runs out to the ambulance and grabs the backboard to use as a skid under the tarp. We get her to the edge of the stairs with the board positioned below the top step. With a mighty tug, we get her onto the skid.

End of plan A.

Before we know what has happened, Jose, cop, patient, skid, and I are at the bottom of the stairs. Everything but the board is on top of the woman, who is now shrieking like a steam whistle. Jose's skid idea worked. Too well. Our patient shot down the staircase like a meteor hurtling to earth, trailing three baby asteroids. We're trying to get off of her as fast as we can, being especially careful not to step on one of her legs.

By now, I'm sure Speed has heard the screams, not to mention the crash at the bottom of the stairs, and I'm wondering what *he's* wondering is going on in here. The front door to the street has been open all the time we've been working.

Now all six of us grab the tarp until we get to the front door, then it's pull/yank/tug again. We need to get the board out from under her to move it so we can slide her over the doorsill and down the brick stairs. Five of us go on one side to lift while Jose yanks the board out and puts it in place under the bottom of the tarp and over the sill. We pull. Now she's out on the stoop.

226

Our stretcher has folding side arms, and when they're down, it can be made to lie completely flat. We will use the backboard as a ramp to get her down the steps and onto the stretcher so we can roll her to the ambulance. That works all right, but how are we going to get her onto the floor of the ambulance. By now, the backboard appears to be the hero of the play. I'm wondering how much more it can take. It's only three-quarter-inch plywood. She is on the stretcher, still on the tarp, and we've retrieved the board to use it again as a ramp. We're going to slide her up the board from the stretcher into the back of the ambulance. This may be the hardest task of the entire call.

Only two can enter the ambulance, backward, pulling at the tarp. The other four of our team will have to push and slide her up the board as we back our way through the ambulance, into the front, and out the driver's and attendant's doors. Excuse us, Speed.

Jose and I are the go-in-backward team, since it's our ambulance. It works surprisingly well, even though our exit is a bit ungainly.

Jose and I go back to the rear of the ambulance to take a look. Just as I thought. She literally fills up the entire interior of the ambulance, from the wall to the bench and almost half the vertical area. I've never seen the rear end of the ambulance sag like this. I wheel the stretcher up to the house, where our patient's husband is more than happy to hold it for us and also grateful we were able to get his wife out of the house for treatment. He obviously loves her very much, and I hope he thinks we handled her with enough care. She screamed so much. I want to tell him it couldn't be helped. I think he knows.

I tell the EMS guys we'll save their tarp for them at St. John's. Our patient is quiet now, and I think she believes me when I tell her the worst is over. Jose, Speed, and I are off to EGH.

Speed is dumbfounded. As much as I want to explain to him that this is no ordinary call, that it's not always like this, that we don't always make our patients scream, I'm too tired to say anything at this point.

When we get to EGH, we go in for a gurney and some help. We tell the four orderlies who come with us that we have a very large patient who is too heavy for the two of us to move. I'll never forget the looks on their faces when they come outside.

Once again the backboard serves us well. Archimedes, I love you, man. The six of us have little difficulty sliding the woman out of the bus, onto the backboard/ramp, and on top of the gurney. The difficulty comes in *keeping her on top of* the gurney. She's so big that she's literally hanging over both sides, threatening to fall off either one way or the other. This didn't seem too much of a problem when we had her on the stretcher, which is low to the ground, but the gurney is considerably higher and the whole situation is much more precarious.

From here on into the Elmhurst ER, it's a balancing

act, trying to keep her centered on the gurney while straining to move her immense bulk. Slow and steady. Nice and slow. Okay, EGH people, she's all yours now.

She's in. Now it's back to her house to get our stretcher. Then on to the Lemon Ice King. We must have made an impression on Speed.

He says it's his treat.

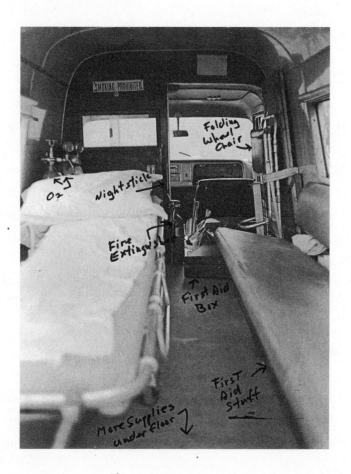

BON VOYAGE, SCUMBAG

THERE'S A GOOD reason I don't like to read novels even when they're superbly written: I don't believe in them. I think they're cheats. I don't believe life happens like that, with a linear plot and a beginning, a middle, and an end. Life is episodic, like a series of short stories. Or even more of an isolated moment in time than that: a poem. William Faulkner said a novelist is a failed poet, and I believe him. Maybe a short-story writer is somewhere in between: a poet who got all Cs.

It may be that the episodes in a life are connected well enough to make a coherent novel, but I have always doubted it, until today. Now I think it may be possible, because this story has a beginning, a middle, and an end.

A really satisfying, terrific end.

I'm starting on a twelve-hour night shift, and it's about 7:30 p.m., still light, but it's the end of August, and already it's getting darker earlier. So it's twilight. I'm on with Lenny.

Lenny is a really small guy. Totally unlike anyone else on the ambulance. More like a furtive woodland creature. He looks like he has some sort of deformity in his upper back—maybe scoliosis. He has what I would call a flatline demeanor. I've never seen him get emotional. He doesn't seem interested in talking about anything in particular. When he does speak, it's unbelievably fast, and I have to ask him to repeat himself half the time. We don't work together too much, but when we do it's at night, and we seem to be lucky in that we often have shifts where it's quiet and we can catch some sleep. So I really don't know that much about him. It's pretty much a pH 7 relationship.

A call has come in. There's a man down, on the street, outside a certain address in Jackson Heights. It isn't a residential address. He's in front of a block of one-story stores. He has been stabbed, and it's a legitimate *rush*. I know exactly where it is. I also immediately know who the victim is, but I can't say how. Lenny knows, too. So do Leroy and Enrico. We had the last call, and this one is theirs. We all agree that we know who it is.

You get ESP on a job like this. You can walk into a room and someone's unconscious and bleeding and his family is telling you what happened and you know instantly it's a lie. The same kind of thing happens when certain calls come in.

These *certain calls* are usually repeat customers. A man with epilepsy goes drinking and has a grand mal on the sidewalk or in the street, in front of his favorite bar. We know who it is by the location. A woman won't take her insulin and pigs out on candy. We know her from her address. Other times a call will come in and one of us will have a premonition. I'm notorious among the ambulance crew for the number of times I've called a dry floater when we get a DOA summons. *Dry floater* is the clumsy term we use to describe a decomposing body—bloated up like a floater but on dry land.

In this case, our experience, not instinct, tells us the victim is somebody we know.

This particular individual is an Asian male about fifty. I believe he's Chinese. Over the years, we've memorized his résumé. He's a merchant seaman and goes to sea for extended periods of time. When he comes back, he and his German wife sit down for some cards and conversation and lots and lots of booze.

After a time, who knows how long, he beats her to a pulp.

I've seen this happen again and again—and I am a mere part-timer. I would not even attempt to guess at how many times this cycle of abuse has been repeated. I don't think she even says *uncle* and calls 911 until he's been beating on her a few days and she can't see or breathe through her nose or the alcohol runs out and she really starts to feel the pain.

They have no furniture to speak of in their tiny apartment, besides a card table and a couple of wooden crates for chairs. There's a little cooking alcove off to the side, and I assume they have a bedroom and toilet, but we've never been farther than the main room, where all the action happens.

They're usually dressed in greasy sweaters and coats, even in summer, which is when I see them. Correction—I paid them a visit over Christmas vacation once. They have one lamp, and they keep the curtains drawn. It's always dark as hell in there, which is okay by me. Who wants to see it that well anyway. I would describe the decor as Mid-Twentieth-Century Squalid.

They look like homeless people, squatters in their own home.

She never says much when we come. Most of the time, she can't. He says nothing. The cops, who know him well, take him in, but I don't think she ever presses charges. We always take her to EGH, and I suppose she takes a cab home or walks—it's not that far a walk.

As near as I can piece things together, this one-sided bout usually comes just before he's supposed to head out to sea again. Once he has sailed, the missus has some time to recover, and maybe they make some kind of ship-to-shore amends or something. When he returns, they start all over.

We don't often get to see closure, doing what we do. This is one of the reasons I see life as a series of loosely connected—or completely unconnected—episodes. We pick people up and treat them and get them to the hospital and drive out of their lives. It is rare for us to learn what happened to somebody. Sometimes we ask, when it's a call that has affected us emotionally. Sometimes we avoid asking for the same reason. Most of the time we try to forget about as many cases as we can, and move on.

I never understood why this couple stayed together or why he wasn't locked up. Even more depressing is the thought that, as bad as things were, they needed each other. He needed a punching bag, and she was *there for him* to meet that need. That's a hard one to swallow. I hate to say it, but I wish this could have been Lenny's and my call. I'm so sure it's the Asian guy.

I really want to see him dead. Is that a horrible thing to say. I don't know anymore.

It's going to be a long wait for Leroy and Enrico to return with the skinny on this.

When they return, they play it back for us, in living color. It's almost exactly the way I pictured it. Make that *exactly*.

They're pulling up to the stores that are right around the corner from this couple's apartment. In the growing darkness, they're following a trail of blood they can barely see along the sidewalk, as if they were tracking a wounded rhino into the bush to finish him off.

Then there he is. The rhino.

It's the Asian seaman, just as we all thought. There's an enormous knife blade sticking out of his back, just below the ribs. Meaning it went through from the *front*.

Enrico looks at me and in a perfect deadpan says, *Mikey,*

it didn't look like no accident. Holy crap. Caruso cracked a joke. I wasn't even sure he could talk.

Leroy says the blade went in at an upward angle, from the front. It went in low. Wife height. Sounds like he got it, then crawled from the apartment all the way around the corner and stopped in front of the stores. I wonder where he was going.

He was 100 percent dead. The proverbial doornail. Not a drop of blood left in his miserable body.

It's hard to tell what Leroy, Lenny, and Enrico are feeling. Three Easter Island heads. I'd never play poker with any of them. But as for me, I feel like cheering out loud.

Well, good for you, Mrs. Popeye. Good for you.

So maybe their story is not a novel or even a novella. Certainly not a poem by any stretch of the imagination. I guess I can't say that it really has a beginning—even though it must—because I don't know that part. But it sure as hell has a middle.

And you couldn't ask for a better ending.

GO FIGURE

IF ISAAC NEWTON were alive today, he'd surely be working in the projects instead of under some apple tree. Things are always falling in the projects, mostly from the roof, sometimes out of windows. Cinder blocks, bicycles, bottles, used hygienic materials. Cats. Dogs. People. You name it, it flies.

Right now, we're on a *big* rush call to Long Island City: it's a baby out a window. That's about as big as a *big rush* gets. I'm on with Sammy today. He can be a really terrifying guy. Also, highly entertaining. He's a wild man, no question, an incomparable two-fisted drinker, a scholar (B school), and general all-around bad boy. Who wouldn't be, with this job plus graduate school.

He is without a doubt the scariest driver on the team. I don't think he even knows that the accelerator pedal has any intermediate positions other than full down or full up. We were hurtling up Fifty-Seventh Avenue on a rush call

last year when the massive hood of the ambulance came
unlatched and went vertical, smashing up against the windshield and completely blinding us at a speed of maybe sixty
miles per hour.

I was terrified; Sammy was jubilant. He must have taken
it as a personal challenge from the hood, daring him to keep
on going as fast as he could. He was actually accelerating.
Finally the novelty wore off, and he stopped and called us
out of service.

And yet, when we have a patient on board, Sammy is
nothing but business—and he's really good at this business, as he seems to be with everything he pursues. I hope
he lives long enough to enjoy the fruits of his considerable
talents.

Right now, I believe we're going as fast as it's possible to
go in the borough of Queens in an ambulance. Full siren all
the way. I hate the siren, but I'm so keyed up that I'm not
even thinking about it. All I can think of is *baby out a window.*
Which floor. What did it land on. Is it dead yet. Must not
be if they put a rush on the call. Central tends to be pretty
careful about this; they don't want emergency responders to
take unnecessary risks. If it's a possible DOA, they'll say so
up front. Good for them.

Look at this crowd. There must be a couple thousand
people here. I wonder how many are here because they
heard about the baby out the window and how many are
just hanging out, enjoying the late-summer day. Someone's

waving to us above the crowd. It's a cop, and he's making the *stay where you are* sign. They're bringing the baby out to us.

It's a baby boy. Apparently, he fell three full stories. Somebody says he landed on a bush first, before hitting the ground. The ground around here is like concrete. What incredible luck to hit a bush. I mean, *the* bush. It's one of the only shrubs of any kind in the entire project. Sammy takes him from the officer and hands him to me.

He has a glazed look on his face, and his pupils are not responding. I can hardly feel a pulse, but he is definitely alive. Aside from some abrasions on his head, there don't seem to be any major external injuries.

But something isn't right. In the code used in the hospital with newborns, we've got an FLK. Funny-looking kid. (It usually means there's something pretty bad going on—not that the kid is actually funny looking.)

Not knowing how he looked *before* he fell is a problem. I've practiced my Spanish a lot, riding with Jose, but it's still not good enough to ask his mother, who is completely hysterical, whether or not her kid has always looked like this. It's kind of a delicate question, and I don't want to risk insulting her. I'm sure we could find somebody in the crowd who's fluent enough to ask her what we want to know, but there's no time. I do manage to ask Mom her baby's name, which is Juan. Sammy helps Mom up into the bus, and I get in next to her with her baby, Juan, in my arms.

All the way back, Sammy is hitting the siren. I would

normally not want him to, with a baby on board, but Juan isn't responding to the din. Or at all, really. Sammy is driving fast but not nearly as fast as he was on the way to the call.

He has radioed Central to tell St. John's what to expect: infant less than one year with possible internal injuries including suspected skull fracture.

I swear this baby's head is getting bigger as I'm looking at it. He's almost beginning to look hydrocephalic. When we get to St. John's, they've reserved an operating table in the OR, just for him.

Two things we almost always do with babies and infants when head injuries are known or suspected: we swaddle them so they can't move their arms or legs, and then we tape them down to the OR table with wide strips of adhesive tape. Even with a relatively minor head injury, where sutures may be necessary, they never give anesthetics or sedatives. Not when it's a head injury. Anyway, Juan isn't making a fuss at all, although a sedative for Mom wouldn't be a bad idea.

They don't do anything at all to Juan, other than get him into X-ray as fast as they're able. Nobody is saying anything until we see the film.

When we do, it's not good.

I have seen my share of shocking things at this point in my days and nights on the ambulance. But I've never seen anything like this.

Juan's skull is a soft-boiled egg. The kind you eat from an eggcup. The kind that has had the top of its shell neatly chipped off all around by the edge of a knife. The top of Juan's skull is separated from, and clearly visible floating above, the lower portion of his skull.

Now we know why Juan is looking strange—and he's looking even stranger by the minute. He's bleeding heavily into the skin under his scalp and around the sides of his head. His head is filling up with blood like a balloon. He has to get up to surgery immediately. It may already be too late—no telling what the pressure from all this bleeding has done to his brain at this point.

It's odd that he showed so few external signs of trauma. The abrasions on his head would have probably been the same if he was being carried by someone who lightly brushed his head up against a brick wall. I have to think it was the fall three feet from the bush to the ground that did all the damage. But how in the world could that cause a fracture like this. It could just as well have been a fall from his crib. I thought babies' bones were too flexible to end up cracked so sharply at the edges of a break. Obviously, I thought wrong.

It's been about an hour since Juan went up to the OR. One of the security guards has come down with the news that he didn't make it. Not a surprise, really, but deeply disappointing nonetheless.

I hate to see anybody die. But a child—I do hate that the most.

I'm heading outside into the ambulance yard to think and smoke. I know tobacco is bad for you, but sometimes I believe it's one of God's most inspired gifts. One of those times is now. Like many of his gifts, it's a double-edged sword.

Let me see if I can begin to figure this out. You've got Sammy who thinks it's great sport to aggressively court doom nearly every waking hour, laughing all the way.

And then a completely innocent infant who falls three stories is miraculously saved by perhaps the only bush in the projects, then drops another few feet and ends up dead.

Hundreds of calls ago, I resolved never to ask myself questions about things like these.

But still.

THE BEAR

NEW YORK CITY is really not the the gargantuan monolith it seems to be when you look at it from afar. Get up close, and you'll find it's a motley collection of little villages that have grown into, over, around, and through one another. Just a bunch of small towns. And, as it is in all small towns, most everybody in their particular corner knows the details of most everybody else's business, often in excruciating detail.

They will tell you these details with little provocation. Actually, it's hard to keep them from doing so.

Am I surprised at 4:30 a.m. to see a crowd of a dozen or more people in front of this address, where we've been sent on a possible DOA. Not really, no. Not surprised at all. They're here trying to get a look-see and ready to tell anyone who will listen what they know about the very public private life of the woman who is lying here possibly raped and definitely murdered in the vestibule of the apartment building we're about to enter.

242

There's just enough light to see what we need to see. In the vestibule, on the floor by the entry buzzers and mailboxes, lies the corpse of an elderly, obese white female on her back with her clothing pulled up halfway and no underwear, naked from the abdomen down. Her face is unrecognizable, having been pounded into a mass of purple pudding, and her head is surrounded by a halo of pooled black blood.

From the way her head is lying flat on the floor, it's clear that the back of her skull has been bashed in on the terrazzo surface. Just to be *sure*, I guess. Looks like she's been here at least a few hours. The livor mortis is about as dark as it's going to get.

The police have gone through her purse already, and we know who she is and that she lives—lived—in this building. There's money in the purse, so it wasn't a robbery. It was an extremely violent crime driven by motives we'll never know unless they catch the guy and he confesses and we read about it in the *Daily News*. I've been told that rape is rarely the primary motive of an attack like this, an attack triggered by rage. The rape is more of a symptom.

There are so many ways to kill another person. You can rank them in ascending order of violent personal involvement, from dropping a bomb on a stranger from thirty thousand feet to shooting them from fifty yards to stabbing or strangling them right up close. Or even hitting them on the head with a rock or a tree limb. But for maximum personal involvement, nothing tops a beating for savagery and sheer commitment. It has to be the most primitive way of all to end a life. How many times has this scene been repeated since we came down from the trees, I wonder. How much adrenaline has been pumped. What could spark this kind of rage.

What could ever prevent it.

Maybe someday humans will evolve who have no adrenal glands or limbic brain or whatever primitive anatomical structures team up to create this brutal havoc. Humans who are more like the benevolent big-eyed, big-headed aliens sci-fi writers dream up. Wouldn't that be nice. No pesky endocrine plumbing to ruin your day or anyone else's. No beatings. No rapes. No fury. No scenes like this one.

Does anyone here know what happened. Oh yes, indeed. The villagers have the lowdown, and they have it in astonishing detail.

First of all, they say she was a lot older than she looked when she went out trolling the bars for younger guys to pick up and go home with. *Did you know her personally,* one of the cops asks no one in particular, trying to see if this is just malarkey from village gossips. All heads start nodding and all mouths answer in a single chorus, *Oh yeah,* sisi, *that's what she always did. Every night.* You'd think if they were keeping tabs on her to that extent, they could have stopped something like this.

Where are the busybodies when you really need them.

They even know who did it. Jesus Christ, this is pretty amazing if it's true. And I'm convinced it's true. I've seen it often enough not to doubt it.

Generally the cops know whodunit almost immediately by simple observation—just by evaluating the circumstances. You really can't call them *clues* because that would imply they're hidden. The cops are simply using Occam's razor, although it's safe to say most of them don't know it by that name. It's just ordinary deduction, based on a fourteenth-century English friar's view that the simplest explanation is usually the right one. Two people have a violent fight; one ends up dead. The living one says he doesn't know what happened. Occam's razor says it's the guy still standing—the obvious choice. Anything more complicated—like an alibi—is almost certainly untrue.

The problem isn't coming up with a suspect; it's coming up with enough evidence to get a conviction, which is not always so easy. Of course, there are exceptions, but in general crime solving is nowhere near as complicated as Conan Doyle made it seem for Sherlock Holmes.

Everyone in the crowd, which has now grown to at least twenty-five souls, agrees: the perpetrator is a twenty-seven-year-old guy from Ecuador. *He*dunit. Well, that makes things pretty simple. *Anybody happen to know this guy's name or where he lives,* says one of the officers, getting a little greedy. *No,* says the neighborhood Greek chorus. But he always hangs out around such and such street and likes to fre-quent the same gin mill as his deceased date. Oh yes, and they have seen her with him on several occasions. Plenty of times. Wow. They know exactly who it is, if not his name, his age, where he's from, and where he hangs out.

Good for you, the Prying Eyes of Queens. Put out an APB on the guy from Ecuador.

Anyway, now everyone knows just about everything they need to know, with only a few loose ends to the story. The theory is our victim went out as usual, met up with Mr. Ecuador, whom she apparently already knew, came home, and something happened to cause things to get out of hand. What could that have been.

When I was nine or ten, in Bayside, there was a notorious murder a couple of blocks from our house. A woman had been walked to her door by her boyfriend, after a date, only to be confronted there by her husband. The woman wound up dead. You'd expect the husband to be the killer, but it was the boyfriend. The word was that he didn't know she was married and was infuriated by the appearance of her spouse. He stabbed her on the spot, leaving the husband alive as an eyewitness. In France, they might have called this a crime passionnel, and the killer might have gotten off with a slap on the wrist.

Funny how the woman always ends up getting the short end of the stick.

Is that what happened here. Is that the missing piece of

this morbid jigsaw puzzle. Maybe she had been going to Mr. Ecuador's place, and this time they ended up at her place, and he blew up when she told him she was married and they couldn't play in her yard because of her old man.

In fact, she *is/was* married, and her husband lives *right here*. Right down the hall. Three steps up and not more than ten paces down. Apartment 1C, to be precise. Does he know what has happened. The cops say he does not. Oh shit.

Is *this* going to be interesting.

Somebody who is not me is going to have to go down the hall and knock on the door, tell the husband what has transpired while he slept just feet away, and then walk him down the hall to take in the horrendous spectacle of his raped, dead, and partially nude wife, probably of many years, all in front of the wide-awake-at-5:00-a.m. gape of twenty-five neighborhood yentas staring through the lobby glass.

I would have covered her with a sheet, but the cops said that could interfere with evidence. For the husband, this is going to be agonizing no matter what, sheet or no sheet. I wish we had a couple more cops here to keep the nosy parkers back. This whole grotesque scene is about as bad as it gets.

Who am I kidding. If there's one thing I've learned on the job, it's that any call, anywhere, can always get worse.

I am standing about halfway down the hall between the vestibule and the victim's apartment. I think I may have unconsciously moved here to get away from the crowd, if not the body. I'm quite sure I've seen enough for today. Lenny and I are just about to turn and leave when there's an explosion of activity down the hallway in the direction of the apartment.

It's dark in the hall but not dark enough not to see what may be one of the largest men I've ever laid eyes on barreling down the hall straight at me. It's the husband, and he is very, very upset. Give me a second, buddy, I'll be glad to get out of your way.

All I can think of is my National Geographic book *Wild Animals of North America*, which shows ancient cave dwellers being attacked by a giant cave bear, at least half again as big as a modern Kodiak bear. This man is channeling that bear.

I'm trying to flatten my back against the wall, the way the prisoners do in the movies, but I simply cannot get flat enough. He literally fills up the hall. I don't think it matters what I do, because he has just enclosed my right forearm in a hand the size of a Polish ham. My God, what a grip. I've never felt anything like it. He's dragging me down the hall with him. His hand is beginning to tighten and twist.

I'm pretty sure—I hope—he can't twist my arm completely off. But not so sure he can't dislocate my elbow or shoulder. From the feel of it, I could easily end up with spiral fractures of the radius and ulna. The kind of fractures abused children get. Maybe my bones are already too brittle for that. Maybe I'll just get compound comminuted fractures. Mister, I'm not the guy. Please let me go. I'd yell at him, but I don't want to piss him off. More.

For a second, I contemplate sticking him in the eye with my Parker T-Ball Jotter, until I realize the pen is in the hand attached to the arm which is now attached to him. Just as I give up this idea, one of the cops mounts him from behind. It's the most absurd piggyback ride I've ever seen, but it does have the effect of getting *Ursus spelaeus* to relax his awesome grip long enough for me to wrestle free. With one cop on his back and another in his path, the husband begins to calm down enough to be walked to his wife's body without further incident.

My arm looks like it has been pressed in the steamer at my uncle George's dry-cleaning place.

What a raging beast. What a force of nature. What a monstrous, savage, ill-tempered man. Well, look at the circumstances. Look at his face. Look at his huge hands. Look at his knuckles.

Look at his knuckles.

Look at his wife's face. It's a matched set.

Maybe the young man from Ecuador is your killer, like everybody says. Then again, maybe not. Most people see Occam's razor as a good reason, maybe even an excuse, not to look for more complicated solutions.

But what about looking for simpler ones.

THE PARK IS GOOD

LAST YEAR DAD was bugging me for weeks to let one of his customers at the gas station borrow my tent to go camping. I resisted, because I *really* didn't want to lend it out. This tent was one of my few treasures, held over from my Scouting days, and I never let anybody else use it. It took me forever to save up enough money for it, and I kept it like new for nine years. It's an Official Camper model tent with a roof that slopes from front to back and from the sides in front, to form a flat peak. The flap that you'd call the door is usually pitched taut to form a kind of awning. No floor—you have to bring your own drop cloth or air mattress or sleep on the cold, hard ground. It was a very simple tent, but I loved it.

It is now a year since I gave in and let Pop lend my tent to the customer, a kid I didn't know, who returned it promptly after his trip. Last week I thought I might go camping again someday, so I opened up the tent to check it out. That damn kid had murdered my firstborn.

It was as if he had poured clay inside the bag and baked it. I literally had to chip away at the dried mud to even begin to lay the tent out flat, and when I did, I realized it was completely ruined.

To make matters worse, I discovered that the jerk who had borrowed it had taken it up to Woodstock, which of course I missed, because I was working. Nothing unusual about that. I am always working. The irony was almost too much to bear. The son of a bitch not only ruins one of my prized possessions but takes it to a concert I'd have given my left nut to attend.

Such is my life in summer. All work and no play. Makes Mike a dull boy.

Summer can be hard on kids in Queens or anywhere in the city, for that matter. Even the cheapest camps are outside the means of a lot of families, and the ones they could get into usually fill up way in advance. But city kids are resilient. They turn streets into arenas for all kinds of games. Stickball, kick the can, touch football. Every entryway with more than three steps is a venue for the eponymous stoop-ball. The side of any apartment building will do nicely for a pickup game of Chinese handball. Every patch of asphalt is a box-ball court.

And lucky is the kid who lives within walking or bike distance of a city park. These are pretty much the same all over New York. No frills. Functional and formulaic in design and execution. Lots of pavement and a high chain-link fence. Climbing over these fences when the parks are closed is a rite of passage everywhere in the city. Just like in *West Side Story*. Some things never change.

For the little kiddies there are areas with monkey bars, seesaws, large and small swings, slides, and painted hopscotch courts. Sometimes a self-propelled mini merry-go-round. For the bigger kids, there are b-ball hoops and walls for playing handball—with a pink Spaldeen of course.

Handball is my personal favorite. I myself didn't know there was such a game as four-wall handball, played with a very hard nasty little black ball, until I went to college. I love it. It's fast and furious, but Jesus, that ball hurts when you're three feet from the wall and it comes bouncing off and smacks you right in the nose or the boy parts.

We're on the way to one of these concrete summer camps in Corona right now. Apparently a kid has fallen on some glass, and he's bleeding quite a bit. It's unusual for a caller to provide this much information, and actually very helpful. Whoever called it in was smart. We didn't get it as a rush, but because of the bleeding, Jose and I are moving a little faster than normal.

I can tell by the circle of kids this is the place. Also by the two police cars (where one is needed). It looks like some kind of day camp, but I don't think it's the Y or anything like that. Maybe a church group. No matching group T-shirts. There are a couple of counselors about my age and maybe thirty kids. The counselors do have matching tees that simply say COUNSELOR. One of the kids is sitting on the ground with a nasty gash across his knee. He's bloody but seems alert, and the bleeding is more like oozing now.

The four cops and I are white. Jose is Hispanic. Everyone else is black. This could explain the two cars.

Things are racially tense everywhere in America this summer. Last summer. Every summer since I've been on the streets working for St. John's. And long before that. But especially since they shot Martin Luther King Jr. two years ago.

This is Corona, on the border of East Elmhurst, Malcolm X's old neighborhood. The police see Black Panthers on every corner, in every doorway, and behind every tree. They're afraid. If they see more than a couple of black men together on the street, they get paranoid. They call for more cops.

The residents tend to overreact when they see the cops overreact, and so it goes. There's always the possibility that all this overreacting can turn a simple call into a major event. When it's hot, tempers flare everywhere. When two different racial or ethnic groups are involved, things can get very tense. Black and white today. Italian and Irish not all that long ago.

It's hard on everyone. The tension. Earlier this summer

we had a call not a block from here. A teenage kid was beating up on his parents, siblings, grandparents—anybody within arm's reach. He and his family were black, so there was nothing racial going on at all, until six or seven police cars showed up.

One patrol car can draw a crowd in NYC. Half a dozen is mob bait.

And, of course, all the cops had to be white. And, of course, nobody in the crowd knew what was *really* going on, that the *mom* had dialed 911. That her son, all six feet six inches and two-hundred-fifty-plus pounds of him, was pummeling the hell out of his own family. A mob is a mob. They were black. They saw blue. They saw red.

This was a big, big, kid, and he seemed to know how to throw a punch and was not afraid in the least to throw one in the direction of any cop who was foolish enough to get in the way of one of his enormous fists. We were completely hemmed in at both ends of the block. Patrol cars had come in from both directions and so had onlookers. Mom was hysterical and had to be very conflicted. Yes, her son was pounding her family to pieces. But no, she didn't want him hurt by the cops. The cops were hysterical and had to be very conflicted as well. Yes, we have to subdue this guy. No, we don't want our jaws broken. Yes, we don't want to hurt this kid in front of his mother and the neighbors. No, we don't want to start a race riot.

No one in the crowd seemed at all conflicted. They

wanted to see the cops the hell out of there or know the reason why.

As fate would have it, none of the policemen responding to this call looked very imposing. Appearances mean so much when you're trying to keep things from escalating. Bluffing is as useful a skill on the street as it is in poker. I could see why they kept calling for backup. But it was pointless. Every new car that came brought more cops of the unthreatening variety. Nobody bigger than, say, five foot eight. Not that this is pathologically small for a cop or for anyone else. But it looks teeny when you're confronted by a guy who's six foot six.

Big Al and I were trying to keep on the fringe of things until we were needed. I wanted to see if any family members wanted help, after this kid had had his way with them.

But we were more or less locked in place. We had driven around the police cars and through the crowd to get close to the patient, and our ambulance now formed the center of a series of concentric rings: us, the kid, the family, the cops, and the crowd, which was slowly closing in. Hopefully not for the kill. Into the midst of this situation there came one more police car. It was unmarked. Out stepped four cops in uniform. The first three looked more or less like the cops that were already on the scene.

The fourth cop was the biggest man I have ever seen. Massive, with intense tangerine hair. Big Irish cop. Giant Irish cop. A throwback to the days when cops were cops and nobody but nobody fucked with them. It was Finn McCool himself, reincarnated in his own man-meat.

As this giant moved through the crowd, it parted for him as the Red Sea surely must have parted for Moses. He slid through it silently and effortlessly. A hot human knife passing through butter. Things got very quiet at the spectacle of this huge man making his way toward us. I wondered where they kept him between appearances. He wore sergeant's stripes, so maybe he rode a desk back at the precinct. I wondered what they fed him.

He motioned to the officers, who now had their hands on the struggling-but-far-from-docile teenager, to bring him to the back of the ambulance. The kid was quieter now. The sight of the monster cop seemed to mesmerize him. Monster cop had the other cops back the kid up, between the ambulance doors, with his butt against the floor. Somehow, telepathically, he formed up the rest of his blue fraternity behind him to create a screen. He said something to the kid I couldn't hear, and the kid yanked an arm free and punched Officer McCool in the face.

We all make our share of bad choices in life, but this one seemed particularly ill considered.

Finn slugged the kid and knocked him out like a light. The sound was not unlike that of a sack of cement hitting the pavement from a great height. And then they cuffed the young man, and we hauled him up into the ambulance, took a cop along for company, since the kid had just metamorphosed from kid to prisoner, and prepared to leave for EGH. Finn McCool got back in his squad car and returned to the precinct with the other cops, and the rest of the crowd just seemed to stand there and watch. Nobody said much of anything, as I recall.

I have no idea what effect this had on race relations that day in Corona. As I say, I'm pretty sure some of the players had mixed emotions. I guess the kid's mom was grateful that her son wasn't seriously hurt by the cops. Although I use *seriously* advisedly; it was a massive punch and could well have caused severe, unseen damage.

I guess the cops were grateful they got out of there intact. I doubt the crowd was satisfied. One thing we'd probably all agree on: it was something you don't see every day. A giant appears out of the earth and subdues a mortal and then returns to his lair.

You could see how myths get started.

But today, it's a very calm scene, as far from mythological as it gets. It's hot today but shady and pleasant here in this park, and I should be feeling good except I feel bad. I'm sorry the kid is hurt. He's such a nice little boy. I'd say he's about eight or nine, and he's trying not to cry, but I can see the streaks. Okay, my friend, let's get you looked at by the doctor. *All right, who's coming with him,* I say. The counselor by his side raises an index finger. It's a combination of *Yes, I'm going with him* and *Excuse me, I have a question.* The question is, *How will we get back here.* It's a good question. There's no public transportation directly between here and Elmhurst General, and he says he doesn't have cab fare. He himself could make the walk, but I don't think it's a good idea to ask the kid to, and he doesn't either and says so. A wise decision for sure. I totally agree.

Without even thinking, I find myself telling him that we often go to and from EGH all day long, and if he and his charge are still there when we've dropped off our patient, we'll drive them back, *if* we don't have another call on deck. Why did I say that. I'm not sure we can do it. I know it's against the rules. In fact, there are days we don't go to Elmhurst at all. So it's possible we won't even see them for the rest of the day.

What excess of zeal is behind this spontaneous outburst. Am I trying to be a one-man ambassador for racial healing, or just trying to be a good guy, or am I yet another guilt-ridden white guy trying to be cool. I'm not sure. I'm not *sorry* I said it. I only hope that having said it, we can deliver. I'm staring at Jose, who says nothing but has that *ball in your court, muchacho* look on his face.

The counselor seems relieved, but I wonder what he really thinks. Is this ambulance guy trying to be a one-man ambassador for racial healing or just trying to be a good guy or yet another guilt-ridden white guy trying to be cool. We'll just have to see how the day plays out.

As it happens, we've been back and forth to and from EGH more than usual today. Every time we go there, we have another call on deck. There is no possibility of driving the counselor or the kid back to the park when we have a call waiting. We can see the counselor and his small companion each time we drive in and out of Elmhurst's yard. The boy has been checked out and is all bandaged up and ready to go home. We pass by them when we wheel a patient in and come out with an empty stretcher. The first few times we go by, I nod to the counselor, and he nods back. Jose puts the lights on when we're off on another call. I think it's so the counselor can see we're tied up.

After a few more calls, he just stares at us, expressionless. After that, he doesn't look up when we go by.

We're still going on calls, but I'm sure it looks to him like we're never going to make good on our offer to give them a lift back. I realize it wasn't a promise, but still. I hate to see them sitting there like that. Don't they know *anybody* who can come and get them. I guess not.

It's getting to be past suppertime, still quite light out, and we're once again pulling into the yard at EGH. The counselor and the kid are still sitting where they've been since midmorning. Jesus, they must be starving by now. I wonder if they've even had anything to drink. Neither one of them looks at us as we wheel our patient into the Elmhurst ER. I won't begin to speculate on what's going through their minds.

But I'll bet they're not expecting what I'm going to say next.

Okay, men, let's go. Let's get you guys back to the park. Hop in. We could drop you off at home if you want.

It's the first time all day we haven't had a backup call out of EGH. They remain expressionless as we open the doors so they can climb in the back. Nobody says anything as we make our way back to the park. Then, *The park is good,* says the counselor. They only live right around the corner anyway.

When we open the doors to let them out at the park, the counselor grabs my right arm at the inner elbow. He looks me in the eye but says nothing. He squeezes my arm hard. Then he and his battered-but-brave little buddy walk away, and we mount up and ride off into the sunset. Literally, into the sunset.

What's it all about, Alfie.

Am I really an overweening white man trying to be cool and/or prove I'm one of the good guys. Is this all for show. I know I can be cynical. Do I have to be cynical about this. Who did I do this for. Them or me. I have to stop overanalyzing things. I need to simplify my thoughts, reduce them to what I *know* that I know, for sure. And what is that, in twenty-five words or less.

I know I feel good about how today ended. That's all I need to know.

STILL LIFE WITH PROSTITUTE

I LOVE BEAUTY. I love art. I never miss a chance to go to MoMA or the Metropolitan when I can. I love taking Barbara to the Met when she visits from Chicago and going to the Art Institute when I visit her there.

I hate ugliness. This is a big problem working on an ambulance in Elmhurst and in this part of Queens in general. Even though I was born in Elmhurst, not more than a few blocks from St. John's, in fact, I have always hated its ugliness.

It's as if a whole lot of immigrant people were thrown into this part of Queens and had to make the best of it with no thought of how it might look. It's *exactly* like that, because that's what happened. Frankly, I expected more, at least from Dad's *paesani,* the ones responsible for the Renaissance. If form does ever follow function, here the function it follows is supporting survival long enough to make a few bucks and get out. And that's just the architecture.

The form people's lives take is equally disturbing, especially when their function is disrupted.

It goes without saying that the things we see every night and day on the ambulance are intrinsically ugly. Horrible things happen to people, and these things are ugly to look at, ugly to smell, ugly to touch, and ugly at 2:00 a.m. when you're trying to sleep it all off and dream about things that aren't ugly.

But it all has to be seen and smelled and touched. People need help when ugly things happen to them. And I do believe helping people is beautiful, if in a purely abstract way. People can't help it when their bodies go bad on them. Or they're injured. This is a kind of ugliness we will all experience, and it's forgivable. Well, it's not really a question of forgivable or not—there is no moral component; it's purely nature's way.

Sometimes I daydream about getting away from all of this and living my life in a beautiful place with beautiful people. In the meantime, I live here.

Occasionally, despite my best efforts to believe it doesn't exist here, beauty comes out of nowhere and bites me in the ass. As much as I try to keep myself centered by clinging to my negative outlook. You can't help looking up and seeing the sky, and it's lovely—disarming—and you realize that it's the same sky hanging over this ugly part of the city as over Oyster Bay or East Hampton.

We're in a very—I mean *exceptionally*—ugly area of

Long Island City right now on a *man down* call. It's ugly to look at and also has an ugly soul. Lots of junkies here. Lots of hookers. Lots of junkie/hookers. And, of course, lots of sleazy visitors and hangers-on, who are always either selling something to the junkie/hookers or buying something from them. It's getting uglier by the block. And the fact that it's a sunny day and just about high noon doesn't make it any prettier.

This is a really ramshackle address, a second-floor walk-up over some transmission-rebuilding business that looks like it has been closed for years. The windows are painted over, and I have no idea what's going on inside, which is the point, I imagine.

I've been in a lot of beat-to-shit places. This has to be in the first or second percentile. There are no colors whatsoever inside the hallway. It's all shades of gray. And black. No white—too filthy. At least one person has routinely moved his bowels in the hall next to the stairs. I wonder if he did it over the banister. You could end up with some serious splinters that way. Do us a favor, whoever you are: don't call 911.

The cops are up here already and clearly not interested in hanging around one second more than is necessary to hand this off to us. They seem to feel it's important to tell us that the man in the wheelchair is the patient and the woman with him was or still is a prostitute. The cops know her from days gone by.

The patient's girlfriend or caretaker or common-law wife—or maybe just a friend—is doing all the talking. He seems too depressed to speak.

This man is named Karl, and he's about fifty-five or sixty, she thinks, and has been in a wheelchair as long as she's known him, which is at least the ten years he's been living in this toilet. How he gets up and down the stairs is a story for another day. I'd say the lady friend is about the same age as Karl. She's very fond of him; it's not hard to tell. And protective. I guess she loves him, if you want to put a label on it. Well, *there's* a little ray of beauty, shining down upon this awful scene.

It's obvious there's something very wrong with this man. There's a lot wrong with him, actually. No doubt he's an alcoholic. There are empty bottles everywhere, and he just has the *look*. The prominent blood vessels on his face give it the appearance of some kind of road map leading to nowhere.

Probably has diabetes as well. That's most likely why he's in the wheelchair. Cirrhosis, too.

I do know that I've never seen anyone with arms that look like his. It so happens that he's wearing a sleeveless undershirt that leaves nothing to the imagination. Both his arms are totally black from shoulder to elbow and then more or less normal, if a bit blue, out to the hands. How his upper arms could be dead and his lower arms and hands still alive is beyond me, but that's what I'm looking at. Last I heard was tissue death starts at the extremities and works its way back. Some blood must be getting through to his lower arms somehow, but apparently little of it is circulating in his uppers. At least not enough to do any good.

His lady friend comes over and takes me aside. It has taken her months and months to get Karl to agree to go to the doctor to get his arms looked at. It's not that he has white-coat syndrome: she says he knows his arms will have to come off. Maybe not tomorrow but soon. And he can't stand the thought of actually hearing them say what has to happen. Would the situation have been different if he had gone when she first started to ask him to go, she asks me. *Really not possible to know,* I say. *But probably not,* I add. Why not make her feel a little better about all this. Costs me nothing.

It turns out the patient is an artist—a painter—and she's his biggest fan. *Do you want to see some of his work.* Okay, sure. She lifts up a drop cloth, and there they are, canvas after canvas, propped against the wall. Dozens. It's amazing work. He paints very much like Renoir to my eye, but they're not attempts at forgeries or copies—it's Renoir's style but not his subject matter. The paintings are all from life. Karl's life, which is quite different from Renoir's.

There are cityscapes he has obviously done looking out his smeary window. Still lifes with empty booze bottles. Still lifes with full booze bottles. Still lifes with half-empty or half-full bottles, depending on your worldview. Well, as they say, you paint what you know.

There are portraits and nudes—hard to tell if his friend was the model. This is some seriously gorgeous stuff. More rays of beauty are shining down all around. But the reality of his position is sobering. It's too bad, really. It would be nice to entertain the fantasy of a New York gallery owner or curator at MoMA or a *Times* critic discovering poor Karl's work and giving all of this a Cinderella ending. That ain't gonna happen.

I'm thinking about how his arms turned black. I can see him painting for hours in his cold room with his right arm extended and raised with a brush in the fingers, the blood pooling in his upper arm. He had to be freezing in here in the winter. The booze was almost certainly making him even colder and impeding his circulation. What about his left arm. Why is that the same as his right. Was he ambidextrous. Did he rest his left hand on the top of the canvas while he was painting. Or was it just his luck to be stricken in both his arms, to lose the use of the tools he needs to create his exceptional art.

I tell his friend that I'm impressed by Karl's work, and it's no act. She knows it isn't. Street people can sniff out bullshit ten miles away, and it never pays to try to shine them on. Big Al and I are ready to very gently carry Karl in his wheelchair down the stairs out to the ambulance.

Do you want to come with Karl, I ask his friend. I don't know her name and I should have asked, but now it's too awkward for both of us. She does want to come. Fine. I help her in. I take a second to look at the squalor all around us. She seems to want to say something before I close the door and we start off. There are tears in her eyes as she speaks.

You know, she says, *this is a beautiful man. This man paints like a dream. He's a beautiful man.*

That's beauty enough even for me.

JFK

September 1970

I DON'T LIKE flying. For one thing, I'm afraid of heights. For another, I'm claustrophobic. Worst of all, I hate turbulence. I can't stand jerky rides at amusement parks. The height plus the violent motion makes me freak out.

On my first airplane flight, in a Boeing 707, we hit some turbulence. I didn't know if it was bad or not because, as I say, it was my first time. It was my good fortune to be sitting next to some guy going home on leave from the air force. He could see I was going nuts.

He struck up a conversation about flying and planes and turbulence.

I was certain he was going to tell me how this was perfectly normal and I shouldn't worry and that aircraft were incredibly strong and overbuilt just to take turbulence many times greater than what we were experiencing now.

Instead, this asshole spent a good twenty minutes describing to me in horrific detail how planes such as the very one we were sitting in could break up just like *that* in turbulence just like *this*. He emphasized the words *that* and *this* like the word *gotcha* in a campfire ghost story. What a jackass. I've never forgotten what he told me about the structural weaknesses in various airframes, and to this day I can't go through a turbulent patch without expecting to see a broken-off engine or hunk of wing go hurtling past my window.

I knew he was being a malicious son of a bitch. To get even, I asked him if he had been to Vietnam and did he see much action. He never said another word the whole flight. My guess—a clerk on a domestic US base and the nearest he'd been to real danger was being on the wrong side in a bar fight. I wish I could say I took some pleasure in this feeble attempt to lop off his manhood, but I was frankly too terrified to enjoy myself.

Some of these things are going through my head, these things about flying, as Pete and I are sitting in traffic, headed south on the Van Wyck, to a plane crash at JFK. I'm thinking about the pictures I've seen of crashes, of crash victims. About the horror of spiraling slowly from the sky and the certain knowledge of the death that's coming up to meet you.

I try not to be afraid on this job, but it's not always easy. There are things you see that no one at any age should have to see, ever, in their lives. I'm twenty-one right now, and I've seen too much already.

Sometimes I try to straighten myself out by thinking of kids in war-devastated countries, concentration camps, even combat. Things like that. There are unspeakable horrors I know I will never see, and I'm thankful for that. But the ones I've seen are enough for me. I do not believe anything positive ever comes out of seeing these things. Nothing. You might think you'd appreciate life more, but instead you're more afraid of losing it. Of terrible things happening to people you love—or just people in general, even total strangers.

But it's my job and I have to be professional about it. There's no other option on the table.

Pete is being his usual dick self, playing that damn *this is going to be the worst thing you've ever seen, kid* game. Like that airman on my first flight. I can take pretty much, though. So far, I've been able to look at anything and not turn away. Anything. It does have its effects, though—not turning away.

The worst so far is not being able to sleep. Playing it all back at the end of the day. Day after day and night after night. And I have been drinking more than I used to. And I used to drink quite a lot.

I also don't give a damn about much of anything, anymore, except marrying Barbara. I often wonder if I'll ever be happy or even feel at ease again. I hope so.

Pete is pulling on and off the expressway, driving at crazy angles over the wet grassy slopes on the side of the road, just to get around a couple of cars at a time. I hope he doesn't roll this hunk of junk. It's so damn tall and tippy.

Traffic is backed up for miles. I have been in a lot of traffic jams on Long Island, and this is the worst by far. It's a big call. I can hear sirens coming from every direction. Probably every available emergency vehicle on the west end of Long Island has been called for this—Emergency Services cops, firemen, fire rescue, the regular cops, and all the ambulances. When a passenger jet goes down, it's a big deal. I can't think of anything bigger.

This call is an *ultra* rush, but we're not going anywhere fast. I wish Pete would lay off the siren. I wish they all would, out there. They're nervous and excited. Doing this for a living doesn't make you immune to the excitement, but it's not a *good* kind of excitement. We need to calm down here. But Pete's the big boss, and you don't tell him to stop hitting the siren. He was having me hit it, but I guess he didn't think I was going at it with enough gusto, so he took over. Go, man, go. See how it makes the cars just fly right out of our way while giving Mike a humongous migraine.

I have read of plane crashes with survivors, but those have to be the exception to the rule. You can't win in one of these things; if the initial explosion or the impact from the fall doesn't kill you, the fire on the ground will. It's all very efficient and virtually inescapable.

I'm thinking about piles of charred bodies and cindered body parts littered all over the place, and I'm thinking this snail crawl to Kennedy is allowing me far too much time to think the thoughts I'm thinking, when, lo and behold, we're here. We're at an authorized-personnel-only entrance that opens right onto the field. There are police cars, ambulances, airport emergency vehicles, and fire trucks all over the place. It's reminiscent of a Boy Scout camporee and might be downright festive, under very different circumstances.

A fireman in a black raincoat is motioning us in and pointing to where we need to park. As we pass him, he tells us to just stand by. Of course. What else are we going to do.

Pete and I get out of the ambulance and start to walk toward the site. I'm struck by the sudden absence of his *this is really going to be bad, kid* crap, so I know for sure he's as tense as I am. I suppose I could sit out this whole miserable event in the ambulance, if I want to. But you have to see something like this. I wish I could tell you why, but I don't have the answer. It's just something that has to play itself out.

And it is an awesome sight. It truly is. The earth is burned black for the diameter of at least a couple of football-field lengths, maybe more. The firemen won't let us get too close, and there's no need to, since they're the ones who'll be bringing out the bodies.

The huge, broken-up pieces of DC-8 are stunning to behold. We're overshadowed by giant pieces of the tail and partial cylinders of the fuselage. There are a couple of engines on the ground and, farther back, the wing they came from. The whole thing looks like a gigantic suit of armor in which someone was burned at the stake. An enormous Joan of Arc comes to mind.

All the other pieces are too small and burned up for me to identify, except for a couple of charred seats and overnight bags.

Two guys from Queens General approach me and Pete and start to talk. They've been here awhile, since QGH is close to JFK and they were probably one of the first ambulances at the scene. I don't know them, but I know that sometimes we all have to make conversation at a scene like this, to do what we can to normalize the situation and reduce the stress level. If Pete knows them, he's not making any introductions.

They're telling Pete and me the story as they've heard it from someone who heard it from someone who might have been an alleged eyewitness. The jet took off normally but never got very far off the ground. It just flew down the runway at about a thirty-degree angle with wheels extended and flaps down, a few hundred feet in the air, and rolled over and touched the ground and started to disintegrate and exploded and burned. That was it.

One of the guys says he heard the tower people were saying that hunks of debris on the runway blew up from the jet wash of another plane taking off just before this one. He thinks maybe a piece of pavement or a blown tire or some other garbage from the runway had gotten stuck in the hydraulics of the flaps or something and prevented them from operating correctly. It sounds reasonable enough.

He says it was a charter ferry flight on its way to Dulles to pick up its fares and take them to Frankfurt and it had a crew of only ten or eleven on board. *Only* ten or eleven. Okay, that's not as bad as one-hundred fifty. But still.

The other Queens General guy says he doesn't think it was fully fueled, since it would probably take on its full load of fuel in DC after it dropped off the crew members and before it was loaded with passengers.

Fully fueled or not, it caused quite a blaze. Just about everything in sight is burned to one degree or another, and a lot of it is still smoking.

Here come the firemen with the bodies.

I know what I *expected* to see, and so I'm stunned when I see they're not really burned. They're not really bodies, either, mostly parts. Impact with sharp aluminum pieces of the aircraft has literally torn them to pieces. The cuts are amazingly clean. Not what I expected at all. What I had expected were more or less intact crispy critters.

Here's an apparently whole body in a body bag. The bag is not completely closed, and there's a woman's foot protruding from the open section. It's a bare foot in a nylon stocking that's torn just at the toe. Such a delicate tear for such a violent incident. As if it got snagged on a coffee table or something innocent like that.

It's a beautiful foot. The toenails are painted light pink. I'm picturing the woman it belongs to; I know she must be pretty. Must have been pretty. This is one of the most pathetic things I've ever seen, this dead pretty woman's pretty foot. It isn't the least bit gory or disgusting. It is just so damn sad.

I can see her getting up and getting ready for this flight. Everything is completely normal. She's taking a shower, making coffee, getting dressed. All of this is playing out as vividly in my imagination as if it were on film. I think she was probably living the life she wanted to live. I think she probably enjoyed her job.

I think she was not afraid of flying.

ON A DAY LIKE TODAY

I THINK A lot about luck since I started working on the ambulance. What it means and why things happen. Why some people get killed or maimed and others don't, neither for any apparent reason. Why children have to die. I see people killed in the simplest household accidents and others survive the most horrendous calamities. You can't know why.

Most people don't even use the word *luck* right. They say you're *lucky* if you have good luck or *unlucky* if you have bad luck. But, of course, it's just *luck* either way. Luck is neutral, like nature.

Some of my hippie friends go on and on about nature, how great nature is, how beneficent, benign, and loving. The nurturing mother of us all. How what's natural is best and we should all get back to it.

I know for certain, after taking this job, that nature doesn't care about anything one way or the other. Things just happen, and that's it. It's ironic that the same people who think nature wants the best for us will then turn around and say things like *Let nature take its course.* As if that's a good thing, even when it's not.

I wish they could ride with us and meet some of the people who are pretty fucking grateful we are there so nature *doesn't* take its course.

Then there's God. Don't get me started.

Luck. Nature. *God.* The Holy Trinity of mishegas. Whatever you choose to call it. Something out there/up there/ around here is making things happen, and there isn't a damn thing we can do about it, other than enjoy life when we can, hope for the best—and try to prepare for the worst.

Or at least try to duck the inevitable for as long as we can get away with it.

It's a weekend morning in early autumn 1970, and I've been working for St. John's since the beginning of the summer of 1967, the entire time I attended Vanderbilt, including Christmas vacations and since graduation in May of this year. One of these days I'll be heading off for army basic training, but as of today, I still haven't heard when. But I *have* heard that even though it's the National Guard, it's possible we may be activated and sent right to Vietnam. It's all feeling like a bad dream I'm never going to wake up from.

In the meantime, I can't get a real job. Or an apartment. Or married. Barbara is back in Chicago, in graduate school at Northwestern. She hates it. We just want to get married and run away somewhere. Any damn where. We both feel like a couple of flies caught in amber.

I can't say how many calls I've been on. It could be thousands.

This job has made me harder about some things and more terrified about others. I just cannot come to grips with the reality of death. Who can. I haven't developed the least degree of immunity against the fears we all share. If anything, my fears may have a bit more dimension than other people's now. Otherwise, they're basically the same.

It's a beautiful day today, but that doesn't keep me from my usual introverted regimen of self-pity, doubt, fear about the future, and free-ranging dysphoria. I think I have learned the trick of letting pain and pleasure co-exist, though. No reason I can't feel bad and pretend to enjoy this wonderful day at the same time. Who's going to know but me.

It's been hot and muggy lately, but today is cool and dry. This is the kind of day when you see lots of cars broken down by the side of the road, with white smoke billowing out from under the hood. Something about the thermostats. They always seem to go crazy when the seasons change. Dad explained to me once how they could get stuck, but it went in one ear and out the other. Anyway, it happens.

It's almost like the cars can't deal with the nicer weather and something inside of them just pops.

Fred and I are on the way to a possible DOA on the street in Forest Hills. What a shame to die on a day like this. But ask yourself: What would be a good day. Imagine if you had to pick your day to die. Or even just knowing the day. Who could live with that.

One of my Jewish friends from Bayside High School once shared with me a riddle from the Talmud. *What day should you atone for your sins,* he asked. I shrugged. *The day before you die,* he replied. Without a moment's hesitation, I laughed and said, *How the hell are you supposed to know when that is,* and almost before I could finish I realized what a dumb question that was. I walked right into it. My friend just smiled. A little smugly, but it was okay. Anyway, I got the point. You will almost certainly not see it coming, so you'd better be ready right now. As ready as you *can* be.

There are a lot of people here on the street for this hour of the morning. The cops are telling us that it's all one family. Big family. Apparently they were out for a stroll, and the family patriarch just dropped dead on the sidewalk. I have had a look at him, and he is indeed dead. Everyone is very upset but not hysterical. One of the women turns to me and asks, *Why did he have to die on such a beautiful day.* Jesus, was I thinking out loud.

I don't think it has been more than a couple of hours since our Forest Hills DOA on the street. We get another call. It's another possible DOA. Also on the street. Also in Forest Hills. Not more than a block from the first.

It's a carbon copy of the first call. Large family. Dead patriarch. Almost certainly a heart attack or stroke or something quick and clean like that. Same trip to the morgue. Similar remarks about the irony of the bitterness of death contrasted against the blissfulness of the day. I don't know about Fred, but I'm getting a little creeped out. But I'll take creeped out over depressed any day.

We barely have had time to get into 434 after leaving our latest passenger at the morgue when another call comes in. Do I even have to say what it is at this point.

I'm starting to think about luck again.

What are the odds that something like this—the death of three men out walking with their loving families on a perfect day—could happen within hours of one another, in almost exactly the same spot. Did their thermostats pop because of the nice weather.

Did Mother Nature decide she wanted them back at this precise instant in time.

Or did God harvest this crop at the moment of perfect ripeness, when these men's lives couldn't possibly get any better. Only worse. When there was not one single thing left to gain by staying a minute longer.

This is a lot to take in. I think I'm going to be thinking about it for a long time.

Like the rest of my life.

A COLD DAY IN HELL

January 1971

I'm on my way to say goodbye to whoever is around in the ER at St. John's. In a couple of days I'll be on an Eastern flight out of La Guardia on my way to Columbia, South Carolina, to start basic training at Fort Jackson. And assuming nothing horrible happens between now and August, Barbara and I are going to be married.

I should be glad that this whole ambulance thing is finally — hopefully — going to end. And I am.

But I'm not that keen on what the coming six months will bring. How many clichés can I cram into the next few thoughts. Out of the frying pan. The devil you know. Be careful what you wish for. Three are enough, I guess. That more than covers it.

Anyway, how bad could it be.

It's freezing cold today. In the low twenties. I've been working for St. John's since the beginning of the summer of 1967. All of the summers and the winter holidays since I started Vanderbilt. I escaped working Thanksgivings and Easters by staying at school. School was my great refuge from St. John's. After sophomore year, I barely went to class at all. No wonder I almost flunked out. Thank God Barbara took such great notes.

This last stretch was the worst. From graduation last May until only a few weeks ago they'd never tell me when I was going to start basic. Is there anything worse than an open-ended jail sentence. You want to start your life, and it's not possible. And now it's going to be delayed another six months. I hope I can find a job when I get back from South Carolina. *Not* on St. John's Queens ambulance. Although I guess they'd be happy to have me back. What a comfort. Always good to know one has options.

What do I have to show for it all, I wonder. All those calls. All the grief and the lost sleep and the isolation and the tears. All the horror. The Horror. Queens Boulevard was the river. But there was no Kurtz to find, no destination, just the cruising: up and down the river and deep into all the tributaries along the way.

What *do* I have to show for it. *Seriously now.* No student debt, for one thing. I was well paid, I must admit. I can't come up with anything else. The job did nothing to advance my foredoomed career in medicine. That self-aborted virtually on day one.

Did it make me understand more about life, other than how bad it can be. How could it. If anything, life is more an enigma to me now than I ever imagined it could be, at least at my age. I would have thought that coming to realize the imponderability of existence was one of the many unfortunate perks of old age. You come to the end of the road and you realize you don't really know anything. How silly to think you would. Is it wisdom to realize you're actually silly, after all.

At least I know it now and don't have to be disappointed down the road, assuming I get there.

I'm a lot more fearful than I was before I started. Why. That's easy: I know what can happen. I have seen it again and again and again. You want to talk fragile; that's what we are. Life's brief candle. It sounds so lyrical when you scan it in Shakespeare. In real life, it's scary as hell to see how thin the membrane is between being and nothing.

So what *do* I have to show for it. Nothing. That's it. Not

a thing. Nothing that actually shows. Try to picture that. What does nothing look like.

When Siddhārtha experienced his four sights, at least he ended up enlightened. I imagine the best I'll do is learning to stop asking questions that have no answers.

I do have a few visible mementos. A civil defense armband. A toe tag I carry in my wallet as a conversation piece. No photos, except for a self-portrait I shot sitting in 434. This was on a day I had decided I'd start my great photo-essay of life and death on the ambulance. Like Gene Smith's "Country Doctor" photo-essay for *Life*. This would be my big start as a photojournalist. This might make it all worthwhile.

What the hell could I have been thinking. Not only would this have been illegal. It would have been immoral. It's bad enough to be present when the worst things happen. It's bad enough to have to see these things with your own eyes and feel them in your stomach and your heart. To intrude on the grief of the bereaved. No need to capture them on film. Flip over a Gene Smith, and you'll find a Weegee. It would be too easy for that to happen.

With those thoughts in mind, I put my camera away and never brought it again.

I also have this jacket I'm wearing today, an official St. John's ambulance jacket. I could have worn my regular coat, but I thought it would be nice to wear this one, as kind of a goodbye gesture. Shows I'm on the team, rah, rah. It was a gift from Eddie the first time I worked over Christmas. A hand-me-down. You have to buy these jackets with your own money, so it was his to give and not the property of the hospital. It's still like new, blood-red nylon on the inside and dark blue outside, with some token synthetic insulation in between. I've often thought it would be more practical if it had the red on the outside.

There is a colorful ambulance patch on the shoulder and lots of pockets for pens and other handy junk, like the foil-wrapped alcohol prep pads I always take along to clean up my hands and the little jaw wedges we carry for seizure patients so they don't bite their tongues: two tongue depressors with gauze wrapped around and in between, all bound up with adhesive tape. Quite effective if not all that sanitary after being in your pocket for a few days. When they got dirty, we made new ones. They were absorbing to make. On a slow day we'd be out constructing them in the ambulance yard, like a bunch of overgrown campers making lanyards. I have used these on many occasions. They work.

I like this jacket, even though it has no vents and the nylon makes you sweat like a pig when you're working. You end up so wet underneath that you don't dare take it off, even indoors, or you'd freeze your butt off.

Everybody's out on calls when I get to St. John's. Everybody I wanted to see. Everybody but Pete, of course. Truly the last person I wanted to see. He's at the reception desk when I walk in, and he doesn't look up, even though he knows I'm standing here. What a puss on. Like he bit into a chocolate-covered turd, minus the chocolate. Now he's looking up at me like *Yeah, what.* He's just staring at me.

No, hold that thought. He's staring at my coat.

Gimme the coat, kid. Kid. It's down to that. I've been here since 1967. I wasn't even legal to work here when I started. They employed me illegally for more than three years. I've gone on thousands of calls. I've been there when he's needed me. I've done as good a job as I could without going psycho or turning corrupt. My nerves are totally shot. And it's down to *Gimme the coat, kid.*

Nice guy.

I tell him Eddie gave me this coat. It was Eddie's coat. He bought it. He could have thrown it out, but he gave it to me.

No, no, no, kid. That coat belongs to St. John's. I need it for the new guy. So that's it. Make way for the fresh meat.

Pete, it's freezing outside, I say. *Let me leave it with Pop and he'll give it back when you gas up.*

No, I need it right now. Lemme have it.

God, is that tempting.

The ER is full of people, and they're hearing all of this. I wonder what they're thinking. There's no one here from the hospital who can intervene. No one who outranks Pete. Hey, I'm in the union, 1199. I pay my dues. Where's the damn rep when you need him.

For a very brief moment, I contemplate slugging Pete. I know I could do some damage, maybe knock him down—

maybe even out. If I were arrested, I wouldn't have to go to Fort Jackson. If I were convicted, they'd kick me out of the National Guard for sure. There's a definite upside to the slug option.

There's a downside, too. Jail and a felony record. I'll pass.

In one motion I take off the jacket and throw it in Pete's face with a hearty *Fuck you, you fucking piece of shit,* the words resounding all too clearly in the dead-silent emergency room.

The jacket probably weighs less than a pound or maybe two. It's like throwing a bath towel at someone, but the effect is far better than any possible punch I could have thrown. Pete looks like he stuck his finger in an outlet. He's in total shock. I think he knows how close I came to getting physical. And in front of all these people. He's a proud man, and proud men are most vulnerable in their pride. I couldn't have hurt him as much if I had slugged him with all my might.

He lunges at me with the jacket in one hand and an index finger aimed straight at my nose. I have to force myself not to blink. *You will never, ever work here again,* he roars. *You got that, kid. I am going upstairs right now and filing an incident report that will go on your record. I promise you, you can forget about working for St. John's. FOREVER.*

Is that a promise. Do you *promise* I'll forget about:

The Forest Hills woman who woke up with a rat eating her nose

The macerating corpse in the tub

The midnight embalming and the *padunk, padunk* of
the suction trocar

The inexhaustible resourcefulness of the suicides

The camp counselor whose horse got hit on the In-
terboro and the cop who wanted to shoot it like they
do in the movies

The shit, blood, and vomit on my hands

The nursing-home slumlords

The bedsores with the dry, white, bare bones poking
right through

The children with the cigarette burns

The endless tears of the families

The lost friends

The lost sleep

The lost imagination

The lost hope

Do you promise I'll forget about working at St. John's,
Pete.

Okay, Pete. As long as you promise.

ACKNOWLEDGMENTS

To Barbara: My infinite thanks and love. So glad we met.

To Emily, Sally, and Charlotte: For the gift of being there to let me take my mind off myself. Thanks, kids.

To James Patterson: I once read that artists are selfish. Not you. *You Funny* that way.

To Jessie Burnett Tidwell: Thanks for all those stories, Grandma. You sure could tell a tale.

ABOUT THE AUTHOR

Mike Scardino is a native of Elmhurst, Queens. In order to pay for college, he worked on a New York City ambulance as a teenager, which led to his decision not to pursue medicine as a career. Mike eventually found his way into advertising, where his ambulance experience proved to be an unexpectedly useful fit. He is married to the woman he met on his third day at college. They have three daughters. He lives in South Carolina.

31901064395165